gluten-free deliciously

jennifer cinquepalmi

Gluten-Free Deliciously

Printed in the U.S. A. by
Aidant Books
www.aidantbooks.com

Foreword by Dr. Stephen Wangen
IBS Treatment Center
Seattle, WA 98104
www.ibstreatmentcenter.com

Text layout by Debra Garris   dgarris221@charter.net

Library of Congress Control Number: 2009903543
Library of Congress Cataloging-in-Publication Data
Cinquepalmi, Jennifer

ISBN 0-9778474-1-9

This book and its recipes have been designed to be a general information resource and an aid to those adapting a gluten-free lifestyle. This book is not intended for use in diagnosis, treatment, or any medical application. Questions should be directed to your personal physician. This information is not warranted and no liability is assumed by the author or publisher for the recommendations, information, dietary suggestions, menus, and recipes promulgated. All information is accurate up to the date of printing. Products mentioned or omitted do not constitute endorsement.

For

my m♡ther

Table of Contents

Foreword

I first met Jennifer Cinquepalmi in 2007 at the national conference of the Gluten Intolerant Group of North America. She was working at her booth selling her first cookbook, *The Complete Book of Gluten-Free Cooking.* We soon discovered that we had a lot in common. Not only are we both passionately interested in the subject of gluten intolerance, but we are both authors who've written about our experience with gluten intolerance.

We spent a considerable amount of time chatting, both about the publishing industry and our desire to help people live a healthier life without gluten. But what I remember most about our conversation was her desire to create quality gluten free food, driven by her love of cooking and her commitment to the health of her family.

I came away impressed with her knowledge and experience with regard to gluten intolerance, and admired her drive to share it with others through her cookbook and cooking classes. It takes a considerable investment of time, effort, and finances to write and publish a book. Now she has gone and done it again with *Gluten Free Deliciously.*

What I appreciate most about Jennifer's recipes is that she is committed not only to helping people discover gluten free foods that are of high quality and that taste good, but foods that are also nutritious. In the world of gluten free eating, I often see nutritional content sacrificed for flavor. This is of course a problem in the American diet that is not exclusive to gluten free food. But, as a physician who focuses on optimizing people's health, it is very important to me.

Although we should celebrate the improvement in health that is gained by many through the avoidance of gluten, we should also remember that the topic of healthy eating, even for those who are gluten intolerant, is not simply about eating anything other than gluten. It is very possible, and I've seen this many times, for someone to completely avoid gluten and still have a poor diet. So, at the risk of sounding like your mother, I want to remind you to be sure to eat a well-rounded diet high in vegetables, proteins and healthy fats.

Celiac disease is an incredibly important topic and one of the most overlooked and easily treated causes of many of the most common health problems today. Interestingly, it is also the only example of an autoimmune disease that cannot only be reversed but resolved, and simply by a change in diet. It is responsible for thousands, if not millions, of cases of fatigue, headaches, fibromyalgia, and even irritable bowel syndrome, which I discuss in my book *The Irritable Bowel Syndrome Solution.* In fact, celiac disease is known to be associated with over 200 medical problems.

Unfortunately, many doctors don't consider celiac disease when examining a patient, and many only consider it in patients with the classic textbook signs of celiac disease which are diarrhea, bloating, abdominal pain, weight loss, and a general malaise and wasting away. Cases such as these are the stories that we often hear about. And they typically involve a dramatic turn for the better in the health of the individual after finding a physician who thought to consider celiac disease.

But a plethora of medical studies and thousands of clinical cases tell us that celiac disease is usually not exhibited in this way. In fact, celiacs may suffer from symptoms that are completely opposite of those listed above and may be experiencing constipation and weight gain, or they may have no digestive symptoms whatsoever, and suffer from any number or combination of, the more than 200 health problems known to be associated with celiac disease.

Studies have also indicated that many people with celiac disease, maybe even a majority of people who are celiacs, appear to be asymptomatic, suffering from no noticeable symptoms at all. This does not mean that they are immune to it or will never suffer any negative consequences from their celiac disease. The damage to their body is still being done. Sooner or later it will begin to impact them in an apparent way even if, for example, it's not until the discovery of osteoporosis at a later age. So the earlier they are diagnosed, the easier it will be for them to prevent problems in the future.

For these reasons, it would be wise for physicians and patients to always consider celiac disease. And, in an ideal healthcare system, everyone would be tested for it. Unfortunately, however prudent that may be, it seems unlikely to happen any time soon. But even if we did test everyone for celiac disease, we would still be missing the big picture.

It is important to recognize that gluten intolerance is not limited to celiac disease. Celiac disease is only one form of gluten intolerance. It is an autoimmune condition that causes villous atrophy, a very specific type of damage found in the small intestine. But many people find that there is good reason for avoiding gluten even though they have never been diagnosed with celiac disease. This includes a tremendous number of people whose test results for celiac disease are negative. In spite of their diagnosis, many of these people try the gluten-free diet and find that avoiding gluten dramatically improves their health. These people with non-celiac gluten intolerance suffer from many of the same problems that are known to be associated with celiac disease.

Interestingly, there are medical tests that can clearly demonstrate a reaction to gluten without the presence of celiac disease. Unfortunately, most doctors are not familiar with these tests. Ironically, we may even be able to prevent the development of celiac disease if we evaluated people for gluten intolerance at an early age. But instead, we not only wait for celiac disease to develop, we usually wait for it to become painfully obvious.

This is of course a very large topic and one too complex to fully explore here. In my new book, *Healthier Without Wheat: A New Understanding of Wheat Allergies, Celiac Disease, and Non-Celiac Gluten Intolerance,* I have provided a thorough overview of the world of gluten intolerance and the numerous ways in which it can affect people. I have also outlined how to figure out whether or not you have gluten intolerance, including non-celiac gluten intolerance.

As you continue to venture further into the world of gluten intolerance, you will continue to find that it is at the same time both very simple and very complex. It is simple in that all you have to do is avoid gluten and you'll feel better. But of course that is much easier said than done, because we've managed to manipulate gluten and process it into hundreds, if not thousands, of processed foods. And as you may have already discovered, even when you do find gluten free food, it isn't always what you hoped it would be. And even if you don't eat processed foods, almost everyone you know bakes with or cooks with gluten.

Fortunately, we are blessed to know Jennifer Cinquepalmi, who not only cares enough to come up with great gluten free dishes and recipes for her own family, but has taken the time to share them with the rest of us. As a baker, writer, teacher, author, and publisher, she has made our gluten free world a better place in which to live. Now you can live gluten free deliciously, and your friends can too, without even knowing it. On behalf of everyone who has benefitted from her efforts, thank you, Jennifer.

Best of Health,

Dr. Stephen Wangen
www.HealthierWithoutWheat.com

Introduction

In my first book, *The Complete Book of Gluten-Free Cooking,* I wrote about my daughter's health issues, our three-year journey to a diagnosis, and the beginning of a new way of life for our entire family. My goal at the start of this new journey was to prepare one meal that was good enough for my entire family to eat. Through trial, error, and some perseverance, my family was soon able to eat the varied, flavorful meals we had enjoyed before celiac disease. *The Complete Book of Gluten-Free Cooking* is still a favorite among my family and the readers who are using it. Acclaimed recipes include the yeast breads, which I worked hard to achieve, *Banana Bread, Teff Blueberry Waffles, Sweet Corn Bread, Chocolate Mint Bars, Carrot Cake* and many of the main dishes. It also contains wonderful family heirloom recipes such as *Big Batch Granola, Spanish Coffee Cake, Chocolate Yummy, and Dad's Shish Kabobs.* Many recipes can be made dairy-free and egg-free since they were formulated during the first two years after diagnosis when my children could not eat dairy or eggs. It also contains a basic education for those new to the gluten-free lifestyle including information about alternative grains, kitchen tips, and valuable resources. It has been praised for using "common ingredients" and offering "recipes that work the first time you try them" as well as "recipes that are simple to prepare." You can learn more about *The Complete Book of Gluten-Free Cooking* or place an order at www.aidantbooks.com.

Seven years later, my family celebrates this diet for the restored health it offers as well as renewed energy, increased stamina, and a remarkably better resistance to illness. We have enjoyed "discovering" all the wonderful alternative grains available to celiacs, most of which are now staples in our diet. (Read more about these grains on page 15.) My children are content, having been educated about the value of "their food" versus the lack of nutrition in "foods left behind," and they are content because their food tastes great.

Gluten-Free Deliciously, like my first book, offers over 250 new recipes in 23 categories, since so often the newly diagnosed feel as though they are now doomed to a life of dry grilled chicken breasts and steamed vegetables. Pizza is a new category in this book, as is the category *Meatless Main Dishes.* It also includes my effort to "venture out," resulting in recipes such as *Tortilla Wraps* which (alert the media) even stretch! My appreciation of cast iron cookware has been renewed, offering great recipes such as *Dutch Baby Pancake,* and *Gulf Coast Jambalaya.* And, because I have children, there are gluten-free éclairs, new cakes, great muffins, easy main dishes, and tasty breakfasts. Most recipes are simple, with common ingredients; some recipes are special occasion recipes and are definitely worth the extra effort (don't miss out on *Southwestern Chicken-Corn Cakes,* pictured on the back cover!). But all of the recipes are tried and true, the food our family eats every day. From my family to yours, eat well and enjoy your gluten-free diet!

What is Celiac Disease?

The University of Chicago's Celiac Disease Center defines celiac disease as "an inherited autoimmune disease that affects more than 3 million Americans. The disease affects the digestive process of the small intestine and is triggered by the consumption of gluten--a protein found in wheat, barley and rye. Celiac disease causes an abnormal response to gluten ingestion: the immune system attacks the small intestine, inhibiting the absorption of important nutrients, destroying the intestinal villi and wreaking havoc on the body's systems."

Celiac Disease Facts

*   Celiac disease affects 1 in every 133 people in America according to a ten year comprehensive study by the University of Maryland's Center for Celiac Disease Research.

*   Celiac disease is believed by doctors to be the most misdiagnosed and under diagnosed disease in America today.

*   Celiac disease is more common than cystic fibrosis, ulcerative colitis, and crohn's disease combined.

*   Ninety-seven percent of people with celiac disease are undiagnosed.

*   Undiagnosed celiac patients are at greater risk for other serious diseases.

*   The average time for a correct diagnosis in the United States is 9 - 11 years and the delay in diagnosis increases the chances of developing other autoimmune disorders, such as diabetes.

*   Even traces of gluten are harmful for the celiac.

*   Gastrointestinal lymphoma (cancer) is about 40 times more common in untreated celiacs than the general population, and the mortality rate for celiacs who are undiagnosed, or continue to eat gluten, is twice that of the general population.

Classic Symptoms of Celiac Disease

The University of Chicago Celiac Disease Center says, "Celiac disease presents with as many as 300 different symptoms, many of them subtle and seemingly unrelated. Yet, a significant percentage of people with celiac disease have no symptoms at all. People without symptoms are at the same risk for the complications associated with celiac disease."

*   Diarrhea

- Constipation
- Oily or greasy stools
- Foul smelling stools
- Vomiting
- Pain in the joints
- Failure to grow
- Weight loss
- Lack of a desire to eat
- Distended abdomen
- Poor muscle tone
- Irritability
- Anxiety
- Tingling or numbness in legs
- Bone pain
- Iron deficiency anemia
- Dental disorders such as no enamel on teeth or ridges on teeth
- Delayed onset of puberty
- Rickets/osteoporosis
- Dermatitis herpetiformis.

Associated Conditions (those conditions that may develop when a person with CD remains undiagnosed or continues to eat gluten)

- ADD or ADHD
- Autistic-type behavior
- Bone pain
- Canker sores
- Central and peripheral nervous system disorders
- Chronic fatigue
- Delayed onset of menstrual cycle
- Early menopause
- Emotional and behavioral disturbances such as depression, irritability, lack of ability to concentrate, even schizophrenic behaviors
- Epilepsy
- Fibromyalgia
- Headaches
- Infertility
- Internal hemorrhaging
- Lactose intolerance
- Osteoporosis
- Pancreatic diseases or disorders
- Shortened life expectancy

Most Common Misdiagnoses

- Irritable bowel syndrome
- Chronic fatigue syndrome
- Lactose intolerance
- Anemia
- Virus

- Allergies
- Reflux
- Psychological dysfunction
- Diarrhea
- Spastic colon

References:
National Institute of Health
Food Allergy and Anaphylaxis Network
The University of Chicago Celiac Disease Center
The University of Maryland's Center for Celiac Disease Research
Dr. Peter Green, Director of Celiac Disease Center at Columbia University

How should I or a loved one be tested?

All offspring of a person diagnosed with celiac disease should be tested. There is much to be learned about celiac disease testing and methods are advancing rapidly, such as cameras that enable doctors to better see all areas of the small intestine. The following links will help you make an educated decision about testing:

www.celiacdisease.net/testing

www.IBStreatmentcenter.com

www.enterolab.com

www.enabling.org/ia/celiac/diag-tst.html

www.celiaccentral.org/what_is_Celiac_/Diagnosis/435/

www.promesthiuspatients.com

www.glutenfreeworks.com/testing.php

Read More about Celiac Disease...

www.celiacdiseasecenter.columia.edu (Columbia University)

www.celiaccenter.org (University of Maryland)

www.uchospitals.edu/specialties/celiac (University of Chicago)

www.naspghan.org

www.celiac.com

www.gflinks.com

After Diagnosis

The only treatment for celiac disease is to follow a gluten-free diet--that is, to avoid all foods that contain gluten. Persons who have the skin condition dermatitis herpetiformis must also avoid skin products that contain gluten. And remember, if in doubt, leave it out!

Shopping Gluten-Free

The newly diagnosed may need to learn to shop for new foods, at new stores, sometimes at several different stores. But life has become easier since the Food Labeling Act has become law. The new law, which went into effect January 1, 2006 mandates that the top 8 allergens be listed on food labels. Those allergens are milk, eggs, tree nuts, peanuts, shellfish, fish, soy, and wheat. In addition to listing these allergens, the new law has established the following:

Under the Food Labeling Act the following always contain gluten:
* Hydrolyzed wheat protein
* Malt
* Malt flavoring
* Malt syrup
* Malt vinegar
* Wheat starch

The following are GLUTEN-FREE under the new law:
* Annatto
* Artificial flavors
* Caramel color
* Canola oil
* Corn gluten
* Ethyl alcohol
* Enriched rice
* Hydrolyzed soy protein
* Lecithin
* Maltodextrin
* Modified food starch
* Mono and diglycerides
* Spices
* Vanilla extract
* Vinegar (all) except malt vinegar

The following are questionable:
* Dextrin as an ingredient on a food label may or may not be gluten-free depending upon how it is prepared.
* Natural flavors as an ingredient on a food label may or may not be gluten-free. If the natural flavor contains malt flavor, it is not gluten-free.

Shopping for Gluten-Free Drugs

Remember that not all medications and drugs are gluten-free. Research your drugs and medications at:

www.glutenfreedrugs.com

Support Groups

Support groups are simply celiacs helping celiacs and can be a source of information, encouragement, and well, support! Check out the national website for each of the two support groups below to see if there is a group near you. Once you locate a local group, you can visit their website for information about meetings, fundraisers for celiac disease, camps for children with CD, local restaurants that cater to celiacs, and more!

www.gluten.net (the Gluten Intolerance Group of North America)

www.csaceliacs.org (Celiac Sprue Association)

Foundations

Foundations provide information, education, and assistance to those diagnosed with celiac disease. Learn more by visiting:

www.celiac.org

www.celiacsprue.org

www.celiaccentral.org

Subscription Publications

Celiac Sprue Association has a quarterly publication - www.csaceliacs.org

Gluten-Intolerance Group has a quarterly publication - www.gluten.net

National magazine for people with gluten sensitivity -
www.glutenfreeliving.com

Quarterly magazine for people with allergies - www.livingwithout.com

Educate your physician

Many physicians were taught in medical school that celiac disease is a very rare disorder. The following website is designed to help educate physicians.

www.healthline.com

Students with Celiac Disease

The American Celiac Disease Alliance has developed and compiled the most accurate and detailed resources to assist parents with school-age celiac students. The following ACDA webpage responds to the most common questions and includes a Model 504 plan, a sample physician statement, a sample gluten-free lunch menu, and much more.

www.americanceliac.org/studentscd.htm

Genetic Information Nondiscrimination Act (GINA)

President Bush signed GINA into law May 21, 2008 to help "every American feel safe from genetic discrimination in health insurance and employment."
Learn more by visiting the following websites.

www.geneticfairness.org

www.genome.gov/24519851

Remember the Positive Points

I tell my children, "If you must have a disease, this is the one to have." Not only can health be restored, but it can be restored without drugs, needle sticks, hospital visits, or medications. Increased overall health, greater stamina, and strengthened immune systems were just a few of the benefits my family noticed after going on the gluten-free diet. The fact that our gluten-free grains are not refined is yet another positive. This diet also keeps us from eating a lot of food that none of us should eat anyway!

More positive news is that the market for gluten-free foods continues to grow at a compounded annual growth rate of 27% according to the research company Packaged Foods, which means more gluten-free choices for the consumer. Store-bought gluten-free food is becoming more readily available in conventional grocery stores and both conventional and natural food stores are becoming better educated about the dietary needs of persons with celiac disease. Hopefully, store-bought gluten-free products will continue to improve in taste and nutritional quality.

Great Gluten-Free Grains

One of my favorite cooking classes to teach is *Alternative Grains in Gluten-Free Cooking* where I teach about the benefits of whole grains, the wonderful alternative grains available to celiacs, and how to prepare a five-course meal incorporating millet, teff, brown rice, sorghum, amaranth, and quinoa. Here are some highlights from that class, as well as tips from my cooking class, *Gluten-Free Baking for the Beginner*.

Once upon a time...

we ate our foods whole. When whole, a grain contains the germ, the bran, and the endosperm. The germ is the part from which a new plant sprouts and is a concentrated source of niacin, thiamin, riboflavin, vitamin E, magnesium, phosphorus, iron, zinc, and some protein and fat. The bran forms the outer layer of the seed and is rich in niacin, thiamin, riboflavin, magnesium, phosphorus, iron, and zinc. The bran also contains most of the seed's fiber. The endosperm, also called the kernel, makes up the bulk of the seed and contains most of the grain's protein and carbs and has small amounts of vitamins and minerals. Though the bran and germ are both packed with nutrients, it is when the germ, bran, and endosperm are ground together that the full quality of a grain is achieved. Additionally, whole grains contain antioxidants, lignans, phenolic acids, phytoestrogens, and other phytochemicals. Whole grains have been linked to a lower risk of cancer, heart disease, diabetes, and other illnesses, as well as contributing to cholesterol reduction. They have more antioxidants than fruits and vegetables and are more slowly digested than refined grains, putting less stress on the system, resulting in a lower glycemic load. Our family noticed that we felt full sooner when eating whole grains and that the "fullness" stayed with us longer than when we ate refined wheat. This is probably just one of the reasons whole grains promote weight loss in adults.

Only in the past 100 years has a majority of the population consumed refined grain products. *Refined grains have had both the bran and the germ removed.* About 40 nutrients are lost in the milling process and about 7 are put back to call refined products "enriched." Good news for celiacs is that millers are not refining gluten-free grains. The *full* benefits of such grains such as teff, sorghum, amaranth, quinoa, and millet can be enjoyed. Be aware that cornmeal is rarely a whole grain, yet when you eat popcorn, cooked quinoa, or oatmeal you are eating whole grains. The Food Pyramid educational materials have been revised to recommend that a minimum of six servings of grain foods be eaten daily, with at least half of those servings being whole grain. Pay attention to your grains and feel the difference of eating *whole* food.

Favorite Grains

My first book includeds a chapter called "Grains from A to X" which contains a comprehensive list of gluten-free grains and their nutritional value, as well as grains celiacs should avoid. The following list is comprised of the grains that have come to be favorites in my kitchen, along with suggestions for how to incorporate them into your diet.

Teff

An ancient grain native to Ethiopia, teff is a nutritional powerhouse. It is nine times higher in iron than wheat and five times higher in calcium and potassium than any other true grain. Teff is low in fat and its flavor is pleasing and mild. Teff works well in breads, muffins, waffles, and pancakes. Too much teff results in baked goods that are gritty and over-baked goods tend to be dry.

Sorghum

Sorghum is my first choice when it comes to gluten-free baking because it gives baked goods a tender crumb and moist texture, has a mild pleasant taste, and combines well with teff, quinoa, amaranth, or millet. I use it as my all purpose flour mix and combine other grains with it as needed. Another reason to love sorghum is that it is more slowly digested than other grains making it a good choice for diabetics and healthy for anyone. Other varieties of sorghum are grown, some for fodder, which is why I distinguished in my first book that it is sweet white sorghum that is grown for human consumption. In this book, I simply refer to it as sorghum.

Millet

This very ancient grain is still considered a staple in many parts of the world. It is rich in phosphorus, iron, calcium, riboflavin, and niacin. It contains almost as much protein as wheat. It is also higher in lysine than corn, rice, or oats, and, when combined with any of these, creates a powerful complex carbohydrate. Millet is easily digested and is alkaline, whereas most other grains are acidic. Millet flour adds a creamy yellow color to baked goods and has a mild flavor. Too much millet flour can make baked goods dry so be sure to adjust liquids when adding it to a recipe. I especially like to add millet flour to yeast bread; grilled sandwiches made with day-old millet bread are great!

Quinoa

Pronounced "keen-wah", this five-hundred-year-old grain is still widely used in some countries. It is actually not a grain at all but a vegetable related to spinach and beets. It is high in phosphorous, calcium, iron, C, B, and E vitamins, as well as fiber and protein. It provides all the essential amino acids usually found only in animal proteins, resulting in superb nutrition for anyone, not just celiacs. Use quinoa flour in baked goods such as breads, muffins, or breakfast foods.

Quinoa flakes can be purchased in health food grocery stores and can be cooked as a cereal or added to baked goods such as pancakes, muffins, or bread. Quinoa offers versatility for recipes such as soups, salads, and stuffing. Whole quinoa seeds are as quick and easy to prepare as brown rice and cooked quinoa can be substituted for rice in just about any rice dish. Cook quinoa just as you would rice, adding twice the amount of water or broth per quinoa, bring to a boil, then cover and simmer until all of the liquid is absorbed. Whole quinoa seeds need to be rinsed in a fine mesh strainer before cooking to rinse away a naturally occurring residue which can give quinoa a bitter taste.

Brown Rice

Considered the least allergenic of grains, rice flour can be combined with starches to bake nearly anything. Since brown rice lacks some important nutrients, it can be combined with other more nutritious gluten-free flours. Brown rice flour offers more fiber, vitamins, and minerals than white rice flour since only the hull is removed. I do not use brown rice flour often in my kitchen not only because it is inferior nutritionally to many of the other gluten-free grains but also because the average gluten-free diet contains plenty of rice from rice pasta, eating rice as a side dish, store-bought mixes, and store-bought foods such as gluten-free pretzels.

Amaranth

Amaranth is one of the world's oldest "grains" (though not botanically a true grain but associated with the grain family due to its similar composition) and is higher in protein and fiber than any other grain. Amaranth contains B vitamins, lysine, and a good supply of minerals including calcium and iron. It has a mild, peppery flavor and works best when combined with other flours. Though I don't purchase amaranth in large quantities, I do keep a small package in my freezer door to add to pancakes, muffins, and waffles for its superb nutritional value.

Flaxseed

Tiny, but mighty, the flaxseed carries one of the biggest nutritional payloads you can find! Though not technically a grain, it contains nearly the same vitamins and minerals as other grains, while containing more fiber, antioxidants, and omega-3 fatty acids than most other grains. It also contains lignans, hormones thought to inhibit breast and prostate cancers. It is low in carbohydrates and is quite versatile. Use flaxseed oil in salad dressings or tossed with vegetables. It should not be cooked, however, because the heat will destroy its healthful properties. Dry flaxseed can be added to recipes such as muffins, pancakes, granola, breads, and crackers. Flaxseed is also an excellent substitute for egg in recipes, see Baking Aids, page 21. Whole flaxseed cannot be digested well so buy flaxseed meal, milled flaxseed, or grind whole flaxseed in a coffee grinder. Flaxseed is prone to oxidation (rancidity) so it needs to be protected from heat and light. Though its high fiber content helps some people with weight loss and maintenance, it may have a negative "laxative effect" on others.

Buckwheat

Buckwheat is not a grain at all but is a vegetable most closely related to rhubarb. Diets that contain buckwheat have been linked to a lower risk of high cholesterol and high blood pressure. Buckwheat is high in flavenoids (which protect against disease), insoluble fiber, lignans, and is a rich source of magnesium. Canadian researchers published their findings in the Journal of Agricultural and Food Chemistry offering new evidence that buckwheat may be helpful in the management of diabetes. Though I don't buy buckwheat in large quantities, I like to have it on hand for pancakes or wonderful recipes like Flaxseed Raisin Muffins. Remember that many buckwheat mixes, such as buckwheat pancake mix, usually contain wheat.

Almond Meal

Almond meal lends a moist texture and rich flavor to cakes, cookies, breads, muffins, and breakfast foods. Some cooks use it as a breading for meat. It is low in carbohydrates and is a good source of protein, fiber, Vitamin E, and magnesium. Because almond meal or almond flour is expensive, I grind my own raw almonds in a food processor until it reaches a flour-like consistency. Be sure to try Super Sandwich Bread, page 42. This bread was a result of one of my daughter's science fair projects which experimented with the effects of different proteins on the rising of gluten-free grains. Though the bread made with quinoa flour outperformed it, we discovered that the loaf of bread made with almond meal remained moist longer.

The Gluten-Free Flour Mix

Gluten is what gives dough its elasticity and baked goods "chew." Without it, baked goods are dry, grainy, and crumbly. So, we combine nutritional flours with starches and other ingredients to help baked goods have a light, airy texture and hold together.

Nutritional Flours

The first and most important ingredient of a flour mix is what I call the nutritional flour. The previous section "Great Gluten-Free Grains" will educate you about these flours, how to best use them, and the wonderful nutritional benefit of each. For the health of my family I worked to come up with mixes that use the most nutritional flour per starch possible, and still have a recipe with great texture and taste. My mixes are comprised of 75% nutritional flour per 25% starch

Starches

Though starches are important to gluten-free baking, we need to note that they have been stripped of their nutritional value and are high on the glycemic index (GI). Foods with a low GI are a key to long-term health. Many recipes for flour mixes found in cookbooks or on the internet are at least half starch, if not primarily starch. Pay attention to the amount of starch in store-bought gluten-free baked items and mixes as well. Making your own mixes can provide you and your family with wonderful nutrition, rather than empty calories that can wreak havoc on the digestive system.

Potato starch, corn starch, and tapioca starch are the most common starches used in gluten-free flour mixes. Starches lighten baked goods and contribute to their moist texture, as well as produce sugar on which yeast feeds. Potato starch can be confusing as it is sometimes labeled potato starch flour and sometimes labeled potato starch. To add to the confusion, there is also potato flour. Potato flour and potato starch are different in nutritional value, taste, and cooking performance. Potato flour is made from the entire potato and contains over six times as much protein and fiber as potato starch. To make potato starch flour, only the starchy portion of the potato is used. Both flours are hygroscopic; they attract moisture. Therefore, they help to maintain the moisture content in foods, which is important in gluten-free baking. However, while potato starch lightens the texture of a baked product, potato flour makes it heavier. It is potato starch, sometimes labeled potato starch flour, which is helpful in gluten-free baking because it not only helps the food maintain its moisture but also adds lightness to baked goods. For those who are avoiding night-shade vegetables and therefore cannot eat any form of potato, I suggest substituting corn starch for potato starch. If corn starch is a problem, try substituting white rice flour.

Flour Mixes

Sorghum Flour Mix

7½ cups sorghum flour
1½ cups potato starch
1 cup tapioca starch

Brown Rice Flour Mix

7½ cups brown rice flour
1½ cups potato starch
1 cup tapioca starch

Teff Flour Mix

5½ cups sorghum flour
2 cups teff flour
1½ cups potato starch
1 cup tapioca starch

Quinoa Flour Mix

5½ cups sorghum flour
2 cups quinoa flour
1½ cups potato starch
1 cup tapioca starch

Amaranth Flour Mix

5½ cups sorghum flour
2 cups amaranth flour
1½ cups potato starch
1 cup tapioca starch

Baking Aids

To understand why unusual ingredients are necessary in gluten-free baking, we have to look at the science behind baking with wheat and understand how gluten is formed and the role it plays. When water combines with wheat flour, the proteins glutenin and gliaden begin to connect and cross connect, forming the elastic strands called gluten. Gluten traps and holds the carbon dioxide, produced by the sugar, which feeds on the starch in the wheat flour. When gluten is eliminated from a recipe, you inherently have "dry, grainy, crumbly." The following starches and baking aids are added to gluten-free baked goods to improve their texture, create lightness, or give them chew.

- **Xanthan gum or guar gum** "bind" food, helping them to be less crumbly. I have had more success with xanthan gum. Be aware that some health food stores sell guar gum as a laxative so using it in all your baked goods might cause problems for some celiacs.
- **Egg replacer** is a dry powder consisting of starches and a leavening agent and improves the texture of some baked goods.
- **Flaxseed meal,** also called milled flaxseed, is a wonderful egg substitute in GF baking. Simply mix 1 tablespoon flaxseed meal per 2 to 3 tablespoons water. Stir with a spoon and allow it to turn gummy (about 1 minute) before adding it to your recipe. One-fourth cup of mixture equals one egg. Dry flaxseed meal can be added to bread, pancake, waffle, or muffin recipes for excellent nutrition, but you will want to use the flaxseed/water mixture if you are using it as an egg substitute.
- **Plain GF yogurt** helps to achieve a moist texture in baked goods.
- **Acids** such as lemon juice, vinegar, or cream of tartar react with baking soda to help leaven baked goods.
- **Almond meal** is nothing more than almonds ground to a flour-like consistency (achievable with a food processor). It adds protein to a recipe, which is something the yeast needs to help it work.
- **Butter** gives baked goods a tender crumb and helps them to stay moist longer than margarine. However, Fleischmann's unsalted sticks are an excellent non-dairy choice for baking.
- **Non-fat dry milk powder** is added to some recipes to contribute to a smooth, moist texture.
- **Milk? What if I'm lactose intolerant?** During the two years my children could not have dairy I substituted rice milk, almond milk, or soy milk with success in recipes that called for milk. Be aware that not all rice, soy, and almond milks are gluten-free.
- **Buckwheat flour** - Substitute one eighth of your flour mix with buckwheat flour for a soft texture in yeast breads. A little buckwheat flour goes a long way in baking.
- **Important note:** Use dry measuring cups for all measurements in this book, both liquid ingredients and dry ingredients.

Dairy-Free and Egg-Free Recipes

Animal Grahams
Apple Pie with Crumb Topping
Apple Rings
Apricot-Glazed Chicken Breasts
Apricot Habanero Short Ribs
Asian Cabbage Salad with Spicy Peanut Sauce
Baked Almond Wild Rice
Baked Ham with Orange Honey Glaze
Baked White Fish in Wine Sauce
Balsamic Roast
Barbeque Chicken Wings…or Legs!
Basic Vinaigrette
Beef Jerky
Big Pot Minestrone
Bison Chili
Bethany's Mints
Blueberry Almond Cobbler
Broccoli Stir Fry
Brown Rice Pilaf
Brownies
Cabernet Poached Flank Steak with Haricots Verts
Cast Iron Hash Browns
Cedar Plank Salmon
Chicken Fried Steak
Chicken with Chipotle Barbeque Sauce
Chili Lime Chicken
Chocolate Almond Dream Smoothie
Chunky Guacamole
Cinnamon Granola
Citrus Salad with Candied Pumpkin Seeds
Coconut Crust
Cranberry Sorbet
Cranberry Spinach Salad
Crisp Potato Skins
Crispy Apricot Pork Chops
Crispy Breaded Tilapia
Crispy Chicken Fingers
Decorator Frosting
Delicate Crispy Almond Cookies
Delicious Chicken Salad
Easy Baked Fish Sticks
Easy Oven Baked Salmon
Edamame Spread
Fast and Fabulous Pickles
Fiery Asian-Style Pork Loin Roast

French Dressing
Fresh Italian Dressing
Granola Bar Variations
Gulf Coast Jambalaya
Herb Roasted Chicken
Honey-Mustard Potato Salad
Italian Baked Beans
Jam Bars Revisited
Jerk Chicken
Karen's Slow-Cooker Stew
Lemon Fingerling Potatoes
Lemon-Glazed Sweet Potatoes
Lemon Roasted Artichoke Hearts
Mango Sparkler
Memaw's Pastry
Michael's Baked Beans
Mojo-Marinated & Grilled Flank Steak
No-Bake Cereal Cookies
No-Egg Chocolate Chip Cookies
No-Peek Stew
No-Tomato Sauce
Non-Dairy Hot Chocolate
Nut-Balls
Onion Rings
Orange Beef Stir-Fry
Pork-n-Beans
Pulled Pork
Puppy Chow
Pumpkin Seed Tomatillo Sauce
Quick Blueberry Peach Crumble
Quick Warm Blueberry Sauce
Quinoa Pilaf
Quinoa with a Kick
Salmon with Potato-Artichoke Hash
Salsa Fresca
Sangria
Sausage Kabobs
Sausage Rice Pilaf
Savory Sausage and Squash Soup
Sesame Noodles
Slow-Cooker Sloppy Joes
Spaghetti Squash Sauté
Spinach Pesto Pasta
Summer Corn Salad
Sweet and Sour Pork Skillet
Sweetheart Cherry Pie
Thai-Style Steak Salad

Tropical Salad
Watergate Salad
Winter Stew
Vegetable Bake
Vegetable Chili

Vegetable Tacos
Warm Pecan Dressing
Wine Balsamic Glazed Steak
Zucchini Potato Soup

Dairy-Free Recipes (contain egg)

Apple Cake
Authentic Italian Meatballs and Sauce
Bagels
Brownie Bites
Calzones
Chicken and Celery Stir Fry
Chicken with Sun-Dried Tomatoes and
Fettuccini
Chocolate Meringue Cookies
Coconut Shrimp
Cornbread and Sausage Stuffing
Easy as Apple Pie
Energy Bites
Freezer Strawberry Pie
French Baguette
Fried Chicken Fingers
Meatloaf
Old Fashioned Bread Dressing
Pecan Pie Muffins
Pretzel Pie Crust
Pumpkin Mini-Chip Cake
Roll-Out Sugar Cookies
Snappy Side Dish Rice
Soft-Cinnamon Sugar Cookies
Strawberry Tea Bread
Super Sandwich Bread
Lemon Basil Dressing
Teff Bread
Tortilla Wraps
Wrap Bread
Yeast Cinnamon Bread

Cooking with Cast Iron

Sometime between my first and second book, my love for cast iron cooking was renewed. Cast-Iron Skillet Pizza, Cast Iron Hash Browns, Dutch Baby Pancake, and Roasted Pecan Chicken are just a few of the recipes included in this book that "prefer" a cast iron pan. Why, you ask? For starters, cast iron skillets are the original non-stick cookware. Iron cookware is seasoned with animal fat or edible oils to create an excellent non-stick surface that can be maintained with minimal effort. Properly seasoned cast iron skillets will outperform modern non-stick pans in several ways. For example, they offer more even heat distribution, can perform equally well on a burner, in an oven, grill, or even over an open fire. They will last several generations, offer food that simply tastes better with no chemical residues or aftertaste, and are natural and non-toxic. Even at high temperatures, cast iron will not release toxic gases like modern non-stick coatings. Cooking in a cast iron skillet actually adds iron to your diet, as much as 3 milligrams for every 3 ounces of food cooked. The more acidic the food, the more iron is leached from the pan. Iron is critical to human health, especially women and infants. And, less oil is required, reducing the amount of fats in the diet.

Persons on a gluten-free diet should purchase a new pan if your hand-me-down pan was used for foods containing gluten. If you do not care to season a new pan yourself, consider buying pre-seasoned pans, which are readily available. A 12-inch cast iron skillet should get you well on your way to cast iron success. Later, you can add different sizes of skillets to your collection, or possibly a cast iron Dutch oven, great for cooking a whole chicken, slow-cooking stew, cooking rice or quinoa, and various other uses. Try cast iron for some of the following uses:

pan-frying
toasting nuts, millet, or quinoa
slow-sautéing vegetables...especially onions and peppers
cooking bacon...it seasons the pan as it cooks
sear-roasting...the pan goes from stovetop to oven with ease
baking cornbread
stir-frying
slow cooking stews
achieving a crisp-crust pizza

Breakfasts

Dutch Baby Pancake

...an easy breakfast that yields impressive results. Serve for breakfast with a sprinkling of powdered sugar and Maple syrup, or as a dessert with cooked apples, peaches, or other fruit. See photo on insert page C.

2 tablespoons unsalted butter
4 eggs
½ cup sorghum flour mix
½ cup milk

Preheat oven to 425 degrees.

Place the butter in a 10-inch cast iron skillet and place skillet in oven to melt butter.

Whisk eggs in a medium bowl. Whisk in flour mix and milk until mixture is well combined and not lumpy.

Pour the batter into the skillet over the melted butter. Place skillet in the preheated oven and bake for 25 minutes, until the pancake is puffed and golden brown.

Remove the pancake from the oven. Cut into wedges and transfer to a plate. Sprinkle with powdered sugar and serve with butter and maple syrup.

Serves 2

Great Basic Waffles

Make Belgian waffles or thin-style waffles with this recipe. We make double-batches of waffles on holidays and weekends and freeze the left-over's for quick pop-in-the-toaster breakfasts on busy weekdays.

4 cups sorghum, teff, quinoa, or amaranth flour mix
½ teaspoon salt
3 tablespoons baking powder
4 tablespoons packed brown sugar
1 tablespoon Ener-G Foods egg replacer
1 egg or ¼ cup flaxseed in ¼ cup water
3 cups milk (cow, goat, soy, or rice)
½ cup canola oil

Heat waffle iron to 7 or 8 setting, depending on desired crispness.
Combine all ingredients in a mixing bowl. Mix until well combined.
Pour onto hot greased waffle iron. Cook until timer on iron sounds, or about 4 minutes. Adjust setting according to preference.

Note: Most waffle irons, even non-stick waffle irons, need to be sprayed between each waffle with GF baking spray to keep GF waffles from sticking.

Blueberry Waffles
Add 1 cup fresh or 1 cup frozen blueberries that have been thawed and drained

Sweet Potato Waffles
Add 1 cup peeled, cooked, and mashed sweet potato and 1 teaspoon cinnamon

Berry Butter

...for pancakes or waffles

½ cup butter, softened
¼ cup raspberry preserves
½ teaspoon grated lime

Combine all ingredients, mixing well with a fork. Refrigerate until needed

Teff Flaxseed Pancakes

Feel good all day with the nutrition of teff.
Read about teff's benefits on page 16.

2 cups sorghum flour mix
½ cup teff flour
2 teaspoons baking powder
1 teaspoon baking soda
½ cup milled flaxseed
2½ cups buttermilk
3 tablespoons canola oil
1 egg
2-3 tablespoons honey or agave nectar
Butter

Heat a skillet over medium high heat.

Combine dry ingredients in a mixing bowl. Add wet ingredients and mix until combined.

Add 2 teaspoons of butter to the hot skillet, tilting pan to spread the butter. Pour pancakes onto the hot skillet and cook until the pancakes are full of bubbles. Turn and cook 1 minute longer. Repeat with remaining batter.

Serves 4

Great Basic Pancakes

2 eggs (or ¼ cup flaxseed meal in ¼ cup water)
1 cup milk (cow, goat, soy, rice)
2 teaspoons apple cider vinegar
¼ cup canola oil
2 cups sorghum flour mix
2 teaspoons baking powder
½ teaspoon baking soda
1 tablespoon honey

Heat a griddle to medium-high heat. Spray or grease griddle.

Combine eggs, milk, vinegar, and oil in a mixing bowl; combine well. Stir in remaining ingredients. Add ¼ cup more milk for thinner pancakes.

Spoon pancakes onto hot griddle. Turn when pancake is full of bubbles and edges begin to look dry. Cook 30 seconds more.

Cottage Pancakes

These pancakes contain no oil or sugar and are quite delicious. Adjust the flour by the tablespoon for thicker pancakes.

4 eggs
1 cup cottage cheese
1 cup sorghum flour mix

Heat a non-stick frying pan or griddle.

Combine all ingredients in a food processor fitted with knife blade; process until smooth. Pour batter onto hot pan. Allow pancakes to bubble, then turn and cook until done, about 1 minute.

Serve with butter and syrup.

Oven-Baked French Toast

¼ cup butter or margarine
3 egg yolks
3 tablespoons granulated sugar
½ teaspoon salt
¾ cup milk (cow, goat, soy, or rice)
2 tablespoons amaretto (optional)
3 egg whites, stiffly beaten
16 slices day-old GF bread

Place 2 tablespoons butter in each of two 13 x 9 x 2-inch pans. Place pans in oven and set oven temperature to 425 degrees.

Combine egg yolks, sugar, and salt, beating at high speed of an electric mixer until thick and lemon colored. Gradually add milk and amaretto. Fold in egg whites.

Dip bread slices into egg mixture. Place in hot pans. Bake for 10 minutes; turn and bake an additional 5 minutes or until golden brown. Sprinkle with powdered sugar and serve immediately.

Yield: 6 servings

Cowboy Hash

or Huevos Rancheros!

2 cloves garlic, minced
1 green bell pepper, seeded and chopped
1 red bell pepper, seeded and chopped
1 jalapeno pepper, seeded and chopped
1 onion, chopped
2 tablespoons olive oil
2 tomatoes, chopped
Chopped fresh cilantro to taste
1 teaspoon cumin
½ teaspoon sage
6 GF corn tortillas, chopped into bite-size pieces
2 tablespoons butter
6 eggs
½ teaspoon salt
½ teaspoon pepper
1 cup Colby-jack cheese, grated

Sauté first five ingredients in a large skillet over medium heat in olive oil, cooking until onion is clear. Add tomatoes, cilantro, cumin, and sage; stir well. Add tortilla pieces, stir, allowing them to soak up the juice in the pan. Remove the tortilla pieces from the pan; set aside.

Add 2 tablespoons butter to the pan. Add eggs and scramble; season with salt and pepper.

Add tortilla/vegetable mixture back to the skillet with eggs and stir to combine. Sprinkle evenly with cheese. Turn heat off and cover for 2 minutes to melt cheese. Serve immediately.

Serves 5 - 6

Cinnamon Granola

*Big Batch Granola is a favorite recipe among readers of my first book,
The Complete Book of Gluten-Free Cooking. Granola variations are endless.
Substitute GF cereals for the oats or add milled flaxseed, whole Millet, your
favorite nuts, coconut, or dried fruit (see note below).*
*One of my favorite things to incorporate in Granola or Granola Bars is pumpkin
seeds, which are an excellent source of iron and a good source of zinc. I use
green hulled raw pumpkin seeds, called pepitas, but the seeds of all pumpkins
and squash are edible. I pulse them in a food processor until they are
"undetectable" to kids, but not ground to a powder.*

10 cups GF oats
1 cup sunflower seeds
4 cups Perky's Nutty Flax cereal
2 cups raw pepitas
1¼ cups packed brown sugar
1½ cups canola oil
¾ cup water
2 tablespoons pure vanilla extract
1½ tablespoons cinnamon

Preheat oven to 275 degrees.

In large bowl or pot combine the first 4 ingredients. Stir with a long handled spoon.

In a medium bowl whisk brown sugar, oil, water, vanilla, and cinnamon. Pour over dry ingredients, stirring well.

Divide granola between two 11 x 17-inch baking pans. Bake until brown and dry, about 45 minutes, stirring every 15 minutes.

Store in a zip-top gallon size bag or an airtight tin. Serve with milk, on yogurt, ice cream, or all by itself. Granola freezes well and travels well.

Note: Dried fruit should be added after baking.

Makes about 18 to 20 cups

Mini-Quiches

Mix-up these crustless quiches one day and bake the next morning for a quick breakfast. Or, make ahead and freeze, for heat-and-serve lunches.

¼ cup chopped green onion
½ cup fully cooked diced ham (4-5 slices Boar's Head low sodium ham)
¼ cup diced red or green bell pepper
6 large eggs
¾ cup Cheddar cheese, shredded
Pinch dried oregano
Pinch dried basil
Pinch each of salt and pepper

Preheat oven to 350 degrees if using mini muffin tins, or 375 degrees for regular size muffin tins.

Spray 24 mini muffin tins or 12 regular size muffin tins with GF baking spray.

In a large bowl, combine all ingredients and whisk well. (At this point you can cover and refrigerate mixture overnight if desired.)

Spoon mixture into muffin tins, filling each half full. Bake mini quiches 20 minutes, regular size quiches 25 minutes.

Mini-quiches freeze well.

Yield: 24 mini quiches or 12 regular quiches

Pecan Coffee Cake

2 sticks (1 cup) butter or margarine
3 eggs
1½ tablespoons pure vanilla extract
1¼ cups packed brown sugar
2 teaspoons baking powder
1¼ teaspoons baking soda
1¾ cups GF plain yogurt
1 teaspoon salt
1 teaspoon xanthan gum
½ cup pecans, ground fine
2¼ cups sorghum flour mix

Preheat oven to 350 degrees. Spray a tube pan with GF baking spray.

Cream margarine, eggs, sugar, and vanilla in a large mixing bowl. Add baking powder, baking soda, salt, and xanthan gum; mix well. Add yogurt, alternately with pecans and flour mix. Stir until combined.

Put half of batter into the prepared pan. Sprinkle streusel mixture evenly over batter; top with remaining batter. Spread batter evenly.

Bake 35 - 40 minutes or until tester comes out clean.

Streusel:
½ cup pecans, ground fine
¼ cup packed brown sugar
2 teaspoons cinnamon

Breakfast Apple Cake

Sprinkle with powdered sugar and serve for breakfast, or top, while warm, with whipped cream or non-dairy whipped topping for a yummy dessert!

3-4 large Granny Smith apples, peeled, cored, and chopped
½ cup packed brown sugar
2 teaspoons cinnamon
¼ teaspoon cardamom

¼ cup granulated sugar
½ cup canola oil
2 tablespoons orange juice
2 eggs

1½ cups sorghum flour mix
2 teaspoons baking powder
¼ teaspoon salt

Preheat oven to 350 degrees. Spray a 13 x 9-inch baking pan with gluten-free baking spray.

Combine first four ingredients in a large bowl; mix well.

Cream next four ingredients in a mixing bowl.

Combine last three ingredients in a medium bowl. Stir to combine.

Add creamed mixture and flour mixture to apples and stir well.

Scrape batter into the prepared pan. Bake 30-35 minutes or until tester comes out clean. Cool on a wire rack. Dust with cinnamon-powdered sugar if desired.

Yield: One 13 x 9-inch cake

Apple Fritters

These provide a special and occasional treat for my children.
They are photographed on insert page F.

½ cup granulated sugar, divided
½ cup firmly packed brown sugar
1 egg
2 tablespoons canola oil
2 ¾ cups sorghum flour mix
½ teaspoon xanthan gum
2 teaspoons baking powder
½ teaspoon baking soda
¼ teaspoon salt
1½ teaspoons ground cinnamon, divided
1 teaspoon ground nutmeg
¼ cup plain GF yogurt
1 cup unsweetened applesauce
1 cup grated Granny Smith apples
½ teaspoon pure vanilla extract
Vegetable or canola oil for frying

Combine ¼ cup granulated sugar, brown sugar, egg, and canola oil in a mixing bowl; beat until blended. In a medium bowl, combine flour mix, xanthan gum, baking powder, baking soda, salt, ½ teaspoon cinnamon, and nutmeg. Add to sugar mixture, alternately with yogurt, beginning and ending with flour mixture. Stir in applesauce, apples, and vanilla.

Heat oil in fryer to 375 degrees. Drop batter by heaping tableware spoonfuls into oil, cooking 4-6 at a time. Cook 2 minutes on each side or until golden; drain on paper towels. Combine remaining ¼ cup granulated sugar and 1 teaspoon cinnamon in small bowl. Roll donuts in sugar/cinnamon mixture.

Yield: 3 dozen

Chocolate Donut Holes

Crispy on the outside, and soft on the inside, these cake donuts travel well and freeze well.

1½ cups sorghum flour mix
¾ cup cornstarch
5 tablespoons cocoa
3 teaspoons baking powder
½ teaspoon baking soda
1 teaspoon xanthan gum
¾ cup granulated sugar
¼ teaspoon salt
2 tablespoons shortening
2 eggs plus 1 egg white
¾ cup plain GF yogurt
Canola oil, for frying
Powdered sugar for dusting

In a large mixing bowl combine all dry ingredients; stir well.

Add shortening, eggs, egg white, and yogurt, stirring with a fork until well combined. Refrigerate the dough for 30 minutes.

Heat 1-inch of oil in a deep stock pot to 375 degrees. Using a tableware teaspoon, shape one teaspoon of dough into a ball. Continue with remaining dough. Gently drop balls, about 8-10 at a time, into hot oil. Turn balls after 45 seconds using a long-handled spoon. Fry 45 seconds more. Remove from oil with a slotted spoon and drain on paper towels. Cool 2 minutes then roll donuts in powdered sugar.

Yield: Five dozen donut holes

Note: Quality fryers have a built-in thermostat which keeps the oil at a consistent temperature. If you are using a deep stock pot for frying, be aware that the oil temperature may continue to increase as you fry and may need to be adjusted.

Breakfast on the Run

Prepare these breakfast cookies ahead of time for on-the-go breakfasts, travel, or a healthy snack. This recipe calls for gluten-free oats but you might substitute another cereal, such as gluten-free cornflakes or gluten-free O's, if you prefer not to eat oats at all.

1¾ cups sorghum flour mix
1½ teaspoons cinnamon
½ teaspoon salt
½ teaspoon baking soda
¼ cup butter, softened
1 (6-ounce) package cream cheese, softened
1½ cups packed brown sugar
1 egg
¼ cup milled flaxseed in 3 tablespoons water
1 teaspoon pure vanilla extract
3 cups uncooked GF oats
½ cup dried raisins or dried cherries
½ cup chopped pecans

Preheat oven to 350 degrees. Spray baking sheets with GF baking spray.

Combine flaxseed and water in a small bowl; set aside.

In a medium bowl combine flour, cinnamon, salt, and baking soda.

In a mixing bowl, beat butter, cream cheese, and brown sugar at medium speed. Add egg, flaxseed mixture, and vanilla, beating until combined. Gradually add flour mixture, beating until blended. Add oats, dried fruit, and pecans, mixing until combined. Drop dough by large tablespoons onto prepared baking sheets.

Bake, in batches, 15-18 minutes. Remove cookies to wire rack to cool.

Yield: Two dozen cookies

Yeast Breads

Wrap Bread

This fabulous recipe was intended as "alternative bread" for sandwiches...see photo on the cover and insert page B. Start with the basic version, then try incorporating the wonderful nutrition of Quinoa, Teff, Flaxseed, or Buckwheat as you make these time and time again.
Place sandwich meats and cheeses on flat bread, roll up, and slice. Serve ham and cheese wraps with honey-mustard dipping sauce or spread a layer of guacamole with your choice of meat and cheese.
Or, make club sandwiches by cutting the bread into 4 x 4-inch squares. Begin with a layer of bread, top with a layer of turkey and Swiss, add another layer of bread, then add bacon, tomato slices, and mayo, and finally top with another square of bread. Cut into two triangles.
Or, come up with your own variations!

1 cup fine brown rice flour or sorghum flour (not mix)
½ cup tapioca starch
2 tablespoons granulated sugar
2 teaspoons xanthan gum
1 tablespoon dry yeast
½ teaspoon salt
¾ cup warm water
1 teaspoon cider vinegar
2 tablespoons olive oil
2 eggs

Mix dry ingredients (first six ingredients) together in a medium bowl; set aside.

In a large mixing bowl combine wet ingredients. Slowly add dry ingredients. Beat on high speed for 4 minutes with paddle attachment. Meanwhile, spray a large jelly roll (11 x 17-inch) pan with GF baking spray. Scrape dough onto sprayed pan and smooth with a rubber spatula until even and dough fills pan. Prick dough several times with fork. Place pan in a warm area (such as an oven with the oven light turned on). Allow bread to rise 35 - 40 minutes.

Remove pan from the oven and preheat oven to 425 degrees. Bake 5 -8 minutes or until top is slightly brown. Cool 2 minutes before removing from pan. Place meat, cheese, and lettuce slices on wrap, roll-up lengthwise, and slice. Or, slice the wrap bread into thirds lengthwise, and once in half crosswise for 6 individual wraps.

Leftover cooled wrap pieces can be stored in a gallon zip-top bag.
Bread can be stored on countertop at room temperature for up to two days.
This bread does not freeze well.

Buckwheat Version:
¼ cup buckwheat flour
¾ cup sorghum flour
½ cup tapioca starch
1 teaspoon xanthan gum
1 tablespoon dry yeast
½ teaspoon salt
1 teaspoon cider vinegar
2 tablespoons olive oil
2 eggs
¾ cup water

Follow directions for basic wraps starting with "Mix dry ingredients (first six ingredients) in medium bowl."

Flaxseed Version:
Place ¼ cup flaxseed meal and ¾ cup water in large mixing bowl.
Add 2 tablespoons olive oil, 2 eggs, and 1 teaspoon cider vinegar.

Then add:
¾ cup sorghum flour
¼ cup quinoa flour or teff flour
½ cup tapioca starch
½ teaspoon salt
2 tablespoons granulated sugar
2 teaspoons xanthan gum
1 tablespoon dry yeast

Follow directions for basic wraps starting with "Beat on high 4 minutes."

Yield: One recipe serves three people, two sandwiches each.
The recipe can easily be doubled for two jellyroll pans of wrap bread.

Super Sandwich Bread

This delicious bread is a variation from the popular recipe Sandwich Bread, from my first book. Super Sandwich Bread still has the great taste and texture of the first recipe, but this version stays moist longer.

4½ cups sorghum flour (not mix)
1½ cups tapioca starch
1½ teaspoons salt
3½ teaspoons dry yeast
1 tablespoon xanthan gum
4 tablespoons granulated sugar
2 eggs
1 teaspoon cider vinegar
6 tablespoons butter or margarine, melted
¼ cup almond butter
3 cups warm water

Preheat oven to 200 degrees. Generously spray two 10 x 4½-inch bread pans with GF baking spray.

Place all dry ingredients in a large mixing bowl; mix to combine. Add wet ingredients. Mix on low, using the paddle attachment, then turn mixer to high speed and beat for three minutes. Scrape dough into prepared pans. Turn oven off and place bread pans in the warm oven. Allow bread to rise 35 minutes.

When rising time is complete (without opening oven door or removing pans from the oven), set oven temperature to 400 degrees. Set timer for 33 minutes. Bread should be nicely browned on top and sound hollow when tapped. Remove bread from pan and cool on wire rack.

Makes two sandwich loaves

Note: Traditional wider loaf pans will need a longer baking time (37-40 minutes). Hamburger buns bake about 18 minutes.

Teff Brown-Sugar Bread

Read about Teff's wonderful benefits on page 16. Add nutritional balance to your diet by making breads from a different alternative grain each time you bake a loaf.

3¼ cups sorghum flour mix
¾ cup teff flour
3 teaspoons dry yeast granules
1 teaspoon xanthan gum
¼ cup packed brown sugar
½ teaspoon salt
3 tablespoons almond meal
2 eggs
2 cups warm water
¼ cup canola oil
1 teaspoon apple cider vinegar

Preheat oven to 200 degrees. Generously spray two 10 x 4½-inch bread pans with GF baking spray.

Place all dry ingredients in a large mixing bowl; mix to combine. Add wet ingredients; mix on low to combine, then turn mixer to high speed and beat for three minutes with paddle attachment. Scrape dough into prepared pans, filling half full.

Turn oven off and place bread in warm oven allowing bread to rise 35 minutes.

When rising time is complete (without opening oven door or removing pans from the oven), set oven temperature to 400 degrees and bake for 33 minutes.

Bread should be nicely browned on top and sound hollow when tapped. Remove bread from pan and cool on wire rack.

Makes 2 sandwich loaves

Note: Traditional wider loaf pans will need a longer baking time (about 38-40 minutes).

Tortilla Wraps

Although these require some time, they are well worth the effort.
Freeze them in gallon freezer zip-top bags for quick, heat-and-go sandwiches on busy school or work days.

2 cups sorghum flour mix
½ cup tapioca flour
½ cup cornstarch
½ cup sweet white rice flour
½ cup navy bean flour
2 teaspoons xanthan gum
1 teaspoon guar gum
1 teaspoon salt
2 tablespoons brown sugar (not packed)
2¼ teaspoons yeast
1 cup plus 1 tablespoon water
3 eggs
¼ cup plus 1 tablespoon canola oil
2 tablespoons honey

Blend dry ingredients (first ten ingredients) in a large mixing bowl.
Add remaining four ingredients. Beat until smooth with paddle attachment, about 2 minutes.

Coat a surface of a sheet of aluminum foil with GF baking spray. Scoop about ¼ cup of the dough onto center of foil. Cover with a piece of oiled plastic wrap and press into a thin circle of dough. Make dough circle as thin as possible without making holes in it.

Lightly oil a skillet or griddle and preheat at medium heat 2 minutes.

Remove plastic from dough. Pick up foil and flip onto center of skillet or griddle. Press gently on foil so that all parts of dough are touching the hot pan. After 1 to 2 minutes, the foil will easily pull away and you can remove it. Let dough cook 1-2 minutes or until lightly browned. Then flip and cook 2 minutes longer. Remove to a platter and repeat until remaining dough is used up. Note: I work with three skillets on three separate burners.

To reheat frozen wraps: Place a moistened dish towel on a glass plate. Place frozen tortilla wrap on towel. Top with thinly-sliced meat and cheese. Microwave for about 30 seconds, or until cheese begins to melt. Add spreads such as mayo or mustard, if desired. Roll-up, serve immediately or wrap in foil.

Bagels

Enjoy bagels once again! See photo on cover.

2¼ teaspoons dry yeast
1 teaspoon granulated sugar
1 cup warm water

1 cup millet flour 1 1/2 cups sorghum flour 2/3 cup tapioca flour 2/3 cup potato starch 2/3 cup cornstarch	**or**	2 cups sorghum flour 1/2 cup navy bean flour 2/3 cup tapioca flour 2/3 cup potato flour 2/3 cup cornstarch

¼ cup flaxseed meal
¼ cup almond meal
2 teaspoons xanthan gum
1½ teaspoons salt
2 tablespoons granulated sugar
¼ cup shortening melted in ½ cup water
4 egg whites

Preheat oven to 200 degrees.

In a small bowl dissolve yeast and sugar in warm water.

In a large mixing bowl combine your choice of flour mix with the flaxseed meal, almond meal, xanthan gum, salt, and sugar. Add shortening/water mixture; combine. Add egg whites and yeast mixture. Beat 4 minutes at high speed with the paddle attachment.

Wet fingers with water and divide dough into 18 portions. Roll each portion into a ball, flatten slightly, and poke finger in the middle to make a hole. Place balls on a jellyroll pan sprayed with GF baking spray. Turn oven off and place pan in oven. Set timer for 45 minutes. When 15 minutes remain on the timer, bring a large stock pot, half full of water, to a boil. Remove bagels from the oven and preheat to 450 degrees. Add bagels to the boiling water, 5 at a time, turning after 30 seconds. Leave bagels in the water another minute then transfer with slotted spoon back to the sprayed baking sheet. Brush each bagel with egg white, then sprinkle with poppy seeds, crushed pepitas, or a sugar-cinnamon mixture, if desired. Bake 15 minutes or until top of bagels are slightly brown.

Yield: 18 bagels

Herb Bread

Serve as an accompaniment to beef, sausage, pasta dishes, or salads.
Or, serve with a cup of soup!

½ cup GF plain yogurt
2 cups water
4 cups sorghum flour mix
2 teaspoons powdered GF egg replacer
2 teaspoons xanthan gum
1 teaspoon salt
2½ teaspoons yeast
2 tablespoons granulated sugar
1 teaspoon dried basil
1 teaspoon dried oregano
1 teaspoon garlic powder
1 egg
3 tablespoons canola oil

Preheat oven to 200 degrees. Spray a large loaf pan with gluten-free baking spray.

Heat the yogurt and water in a small sauce pan over medium heat until warm. Meanwhile, add dry ingredients to a large mixing bowl; combine at low speed. Add egg, canola oil, and warmed yogurt mixture to mixing bowl and mix on high 3 minutes.

Scrape batter into prepared loaf pan, filling pan half-full. If there is remaining batter, place in another small pan. Drizzle with olive oil. Turn off 200 degree oven and place pan in warm oven; allow bread to rise 35 minutes.

When rising time is finished, turn oven to 400 degrees without removing pan from oven or opening oven door. Bake 40 minutes.

Yield: One large loaf

French Baguette

3 cups sorghum flour mix
½ cup cornstarch
½ teaspoon salt
2¼ teaspoons yeast
2 tablespoons dry egg replacer whisked in 3 tablespoons cool water
2 teaspoons xanthan gum
1½ to 1¾ cups water
2 egg whites
1 tablespoon honey

Combine all dry ingredients in a large mixing bowl. Add remaining ingredients and beat on high 3 minutes using the paddle attachment.

Form a sheet of heavy duty foil into a long skinny loaf pan. Place foil pan on cookie sheet and support foil pan by placing smaller baking pans or loaf pans along the sides. Foil should be the length of the jellyroll pan and about 3 inches wide. Don't over-fill foil pan. Extra dough can be baked in a small loaf pan.

Turn oven off and place dough in the warm oven; let rise 40 minutes.

Without removing pan from the oven, turn oven to 400 degrees and bake 20 - 25 minutes. Serve warm from the oven.

Yield: One baguette

Yeast Cinnamon Bread

1¼ cups milk, heated slightly
10 tablespoons butter or margarine, divided
4 tablespoons granulated sugar, divided
1 tablespoon yeast
1 large egg
2½ cups sorghum flour mix
½ cup cornstarch
1½ teaspoons xanthan gum
1 teaspoon gelatin
½ teaspoon salt
4 teaspoons cinnamon

Preheat oven to 200 degrees.

Pour ¼ cup of the milk in a small bowl. Add 2 tablespoons sugar and 1 tablespoon yeast. Set aside in a warm place to proof.

Mix together flour mix, cornstarch, xanthan gum, gelatin, and salt.

Add 6 tablespoons of butter or margarine to remaining 1 cup warm milk; stir to melt. Pour the milk/butter mixture into mixing bowl. Add the proofed yeast/milk mixture and one egg. Blend together on low speed. Stop the mixer. Add the flour mix, xanthan gum, gelatin, and salt. Restart the mixer on low. The dough will come together and is a bit heavy. Mix on medium-high for 5 minutes using the paddle attachment.

While the bread is mixing, generously spray an 8 x 5-inch loaf pan with GF baking spray.

Spread half of bread batter on bottom of pan. Sprinkle with 1 tablespoon granulated sugar, 2 teaspoons cinnamon, and 2 tablespoons melted butter or margarine. Top with remaining batter. Sprinkle remaining sugar and cinnamon over batter, then top with remaining 2 tablespoons melted butter. Turn oven off and place bread in warm oven, allowing it to rise 30 minutes. After rising time is complete, without removing pan from oven or opening oven door, turn oven to 375 degrees and bake 35-40 minutes. Cool 5 minutes, then remove bread from pan and place on wire rack.

Makes one 8 x 5-inch loaf

Quick Breads

Biscuits

2 cups buttermilk
4 tablespoons soft, not melted, butter
2 eggs
2½ cups sorghum flour mix
½ cup cornstarch
1½ teaspoons xanthan gum
1½ teaspoons baking soda
2 teaspoons baking powder, heaping
4 heaping teaspoons granulated sugar

Preheat oven to 400 degrees. Spray a good quality baking sheet with GF baking spray.

Mix first three ingredients in a small bowl with a fork or pastry blender.

Mix all remaining ingredients together in a separate bowl. Add dry ingredients to wet ingredients and stir with a fork just until all flour is combined.

Drop by large spoonfuls onto the prepared baking sheet, making about 10 - 12 biscuits. Bake about 12 - 15 minutes.

Serves 6

No Egg Biscuits

This biscuit version might be your favorite, regardless of whether or not you are able to eat eggs!

2 cups sorghum flour
1 cup tapioca starch
1 tablespoon baking powder
1 tablespoon sugar
1 teaspoon salt
½ teaspoon baking soda
½ teaspoon xanthan gum
4 tablespoons butter
1¼ cups buttermilk
¼ cup plain GF yogurt

Preheat oven to 450 degrees. Spray a 13 x 9-inch baking pan with GF baking spray.

Place sorghum flour and tapioca starch in a small bowl, stirring well to combine. Remove 1 cup of flour mixture; set aside.

Place remaining 2 cups of flour mixture in the bowl of a food processor fitted with knife blade. Add baking powder, sugar, salt, baking soda, and xanthan gum. Pulse food processor until all ingredients are combined.

Cut butter into small pieces and add to the flour mixture. Pulse until the mixture resembles coarse meal. Empty the mixture into a large mixing bowl. Add reserved cup of flour mixture, yogurt, and buttermilk, stirring well.

Drop biscuits onto the prepared pan, forming 12 biscuits. Bake about 14 minutes.

Yield: One dozen biscuits

Blue Corn Muffins

Bring some variety to your table with blue corn, which offers more protein than the yellow or white varieties. Serve these alongside Huevos Rancheros for a special breakfast or brunch, or with sausage and a bell pepper- tomato salad for a lunch or dinner.

½ cup packed brown sugar
2 cups sorghum flour mix
1 cup blue cornmeal
1 tablespoon baking powder
1 teaspoon baking soda
¾ teaspoon salt
3 eggs
½ cup canola oil
1½ cups plain yogurt
3 tablespoons pure Maple syrup
2 teaspoons pure vanilla extract
2 cups fresh blackberries

Preheat oven to 375 degrees.

Spray 12 muffin tins with GF baking spray.

Combine first six ingredients in mixing bowl. Add eggs, canola oil, yogurt, Maple syrup, and vanilla, blending until mixed. Fold in blackberries. Spoon batter into well-greased muffin tins. Bake 16 - 20 minutes or until tester comes out clean.

Yield: 12 muffins

Quinoa Cornbread Muffins

Quinoa and corn combine to create these delicious muffins packed with nutrition. These are one of our favorite accompaniments to Savory Squash Soup on page 239 or try them with a bowl of chili!

1/3 cup packed brown sugar
1/2 cup canola oil
2 eggs or 1/3 cup flaxseed meal in 1/4 cup water
1½ cups sorghum flour mix
1 teaspoon xanthan gum
3 teaspoons baking powder
1/8 teaspoon salt
3/4 cup yellow or blue cornmeal
3/4 cup quinoa flour or quinoa flakes
2 cups milk

Preheat oven to 400 degrees. Spray about 20 muffin tins with GF baking spray.

In a mixing bowl blend together sugar and oil. Add the eggs and mix well. Add the dry ingredients, alternating with milk, mixing until well combined. Pour batter into the prepared muffin tins, filling tins half full. Bake 15 minutes. Serve warm.

Slice leftover muffins in half and place under the broiler to toast. Serve with butter and jam for breakfast.

Yield: 16-24 muffins

Blueberry-Orange Scones

These scones have a tender crumb and delicious flavor. They are low in sugar and use Sorghum flour mix, which is more slowly digested than other grains. See photo on back cover and insert page A.

1½ cups sorghum flour mix
½ cup yellow cornmeal
2 tablespoons granulated sugar
2 tablespoons packed brown sugar
1½ teaspoons baking powder
¼ teaspoon baking soda
½ cup cold butter, grated
½ cup plain yogurt
1 egg
2 teaspoons dried fine orange peel
1 cup frozen wild blueberries, thawed and drained
1 teaspoon cornstarch
3 - 4 teaspoons orange juice
1 cup powdered sugar
3 tablespoons chopped almonds, toasted (optional)

Preheat oven to 450 degrees.

Coat a large baking pan with GF baking spray.

In a large mixing bowl, combine flour mix, cornmeal, granulated sugar, brown sugar, baking powder, and baking soda. Add grated butter, yogurt, egg, and orange peel; stir just until moistened.

In a small bowl, toss frozen berries with cornstarch to coat; add to flour mixture. Stir gently just until berries are incorporated. Using a large spoon, drop dough into 12 mounds on prepared baking sheet, leaving 1 inch between mounds.

Bake 11 - 13 minutes or until tops are golden.

For icing, in a small bowl whisk enough juice into powdered sugar until drizzling consistency. Drizzle over warm scones. Sprinkle with nuts if desired. Serve immediately.

Yield: 12 scones

Flaxseed Raisin Muffins

Moist, with a pleasing balance of flavors, these low-fat, low-sugar, low-carb muffins are made again and again at our home. Serve them as a healthy breakfast, lunch, or snack. This recipe incorporates healthy alternative grains while eliminating the starches commonly used in gluten-free recipes.

¾ cup sorghum flour (not mix)
¾ cup buckwheat flour
½ cup ground flaxseed meal
½ cup brown sugar
1 teaspoon baking soda
½ teaspoon cinnamon
¼ teaspoon nutmeg
½ cup raisins or currants
2 eggs
¼ cup canola oil
½ cup unsweetened applesauce
½ cup plain GF yogurt
½ cup milk

Preheat oven to 375 degrees.

Spray 12 muffin tins with GF baking spray.

In a mixing bowl, whisk together sorghum flour, buckwheat flour, flaxseed meal, brown sugar, baking soda, cinnamon, nutmeg, and raisins or currants. Add eggs, oil, applesauce, yogurt, and milk. Stir until just combined. Spoon batter into the prepared tins. Bake 18-20 minutes or until knife inserted into center muffin comes out clean. Cool muffins 3 minutes before unmolding.

Yield: One dozen muffins

Peach Pie Muffins

The wonderful aroma of peach pie will fill your kitchen as these bake. Although they contain egg, these muffins do not contain dairy! Try apple pie filling, pecans, and 1 teaspoon of cinnamon for an apple pie variety. Serve either variety for breakfast with a bowl of hot cereal and enjoy!

1 cup chopped pecans
3 cups sorghum flour mix
1 teaspoon baking soda
2 teaspoons baking powder
1 teaspoon xanthan gum
1 teaspoon salt
1¾ cups packed brown sugar
¾ cup canola oil
3 large eggs
1 teaspoon pure vanilla extract
1 (21-ounce) can peach fruit filling

Heat chopped pecans in a small nonstick skillet over medium-low heat, stirring often, 5-8 minutes or until toasted.

Pour peach pie filling onto a dinner plate. Chop peach slices into thirds.

Preheat oven to 375 degrees. Spray 24 muffin tins with GF baking spray.

Add flour mix, baking soda, baking powder, xanthan gum, salt, and brown sugar to a large mixing bowl. Blend on low speed. Stop mixer and add oil, eggs, vanilla, chopped peaches with filling, and pecans. Return mixer to low speed until well blended, stopping to scrape down sides of bowl. Divide batter among 24 muffin tins. Bake 18-20 minutes or until tester comes out clean. Remove from pan while muffins are still warm.

Makes two dozen muffins

Strawberry-Banana Muffins

Yum!

½ cup (1 stick) butter, softened
1 cup granulated sugar
2 cups plus 1 tablespoon sorghum flour mix
1 teaspoon baking powder
½ teaspoon baking soda
¼ cup plain yogurt
1 very ripe banana
1 cup sliced unsweetened frozen strawberries, thawed
1 teaspoon pure vanilla extract
1 teaspoon xanthan gum
¼ teaspoon salt
2 eggs

Preheat oven to 350 degrees. Generously spray 24 muffin tins or line muffin tins with paper muffin liners.

Cream the butter and sugar in a large mixing bowl. Add remaining ingredients, mixing until just combined. Pour batter into the prepared muffin tins, filling half full. Bake 20 minutes or until tester comes out clean. Cool 10 minutes before removing from pan.

Yield: Two dozen muffins

Pecan Pie Muffins

This is a super-easy recipe, best served warm from the oven!

½ cup (1 stick) butter or margarine
½ cup packed brown sugar
½ cup sorghum flour mix
2 large eggs
1 teaspoon pure vanilla extract
¼ teaspoon salt
1 cup chopped pecans

Preheat oven to 350 degrees. Spray 10 regular muffin tins or 24 mini muffin tins with GF baking spray.

Melt butter or margarine in a small saucepan. Stir in brown sugar and remaining ingredients. Pour into greased baking tins. Bake 18 minutes for regular size muffins or 10 -12 minutes for mini muffins.

Yield: 10 large muffins or 24 mini muffins

Strawberry Tea Bread

1¾ cups sorghum flour mix
½ teaspoon salt
1 cup granulated sugar
1½ teaspoons cinnamon
½ teaspoon baking soda
2 teaspoons baking powder
1 teaspoon xanthan gum
1 (10-ounce) package frozen sliced strawberries, thawed
2 eggs
½ cup canola oil

Preheat oven to 350 degrees. Spray 6 mini bread loaf pans with GF baking spray.

Combine first seven ingredients in a mixing bowl; mix well. Then add remaining 3 ingredients and mix until well combined. Spoon batter into the prepared pans. Sprinkle with sugar/cinnamon if desired. Bake about 18-22 minutes or until tester comes out clean.

Yield: 6 mini loaves

Desserts

Gluten-Free Éclairs

This recipe doesn't taste any different from the wheat version my mother made! Fill with pudding made from a mix or the homemade custard below! Consider making the custard filling first so it can cool while you are preparing the éclairs. See photo on insert page H.

1 cup water
½ cup butter
1 teaspoon granulated sugar
¼ teaspoon salt
¼ cup millet flour
¼ cup sweet white rice flour
½ cup potato starch
4 eggs

Preheat oven to 400 degrees. Spray a baking sheet with GF baking spray.

In a saucepan over medium heat, bring water, butter, sugar, and salt to a boil. Add millet flour, sweet white rice flour, and potato starch all at once; stir until a smooth ball forms. Remove from heat; let stand 5 minutes.

Add eggs to the mixture, one at a time, beating well after each addition. Beat until smooth. Cut a ½-inch hole in corner of a heavy duty plastic bag, add batter and pipe batter into 12 strips on a greased baking sheet. Or, spoon 10 dollops onto a greased baking sheet, for cream puffs. Bake 30 -32 minutes. Remove éclairs from the pan and place on wire rack. Immediately cut tops off to allow steam to escape. Cool before filling.

Filling:
¼ cup sugar
3 tablespoons cornstarch
2½ cups milk
2 egg yolks
1 tablespoon butter
1½ teaspoons pure vanilla extract

In saucepan combine cornstarch and sugar; gradually add milk until smooth. Cook over medium heat, stirring constantly, until mixture begins to bubble. Reduce heat; cook and stir 2 minutes longer. Remove from heat.

Stir 1 cup of the hot filling into egg yolks; return all to the pan. Bring to a gentle boil. Cook 2 minutes, stirring constantly. Remove from heat, stir in butter and vanilla. Cool on countertop for about 30 minutes, then refrigerate to thoroughly cool.

Spoon custard into the puffs. Replace tops. Drizzle top of éclairs or cream puffs with chocolate glaze if desired.

Crepes

Gluten-free crepes are easy and delicious.
Fill with crepe filling of your choice.

3 eggs
1¼ cups milk
¾ cup sorghum flour mix
1 tablespoon honey
½ teaspoon salt
1 teaspoon nonfat dry milk powder

Heat a non-stick crepe pan or cast iron pan over medium-high heat.

In a medium size bowl, beat eggs until thick. Stir in milk. Add remaining ingredients; whisk until smooth. Pour dough into hot pan until about 8-inches in diameter. Cook about 1 minute. Loosen edges then turn crepe and cook on other side about 1 minute. Serve with crepe filling of choice.

Makes about 10 crepes

Fruit-Topped Meringues

A crisp shell of meringue and fresh fruit make a light,
colorful, flavorful dessert.

6 egg whites
Pinch of salt
1 cup plus 2 tablespoons granulated sugar, divided
1 tablespoon cornstarch, sifted
1 teaspoon white vinegar
2 cups heavy cream
2 pints blueberries, rinsed and drained
2 pints raspberries, rinsed and drained
1 pound strawberries, rinsed, cored, and sliced

Whip the cream with 2 tablespoons sugar until peaks form; refrigerate.

Preheat oven to 250 degrees. Line two baking sheets with parchment paper. Whip egg whites with mixer until stiff peaks form, about 5 minutes. Add salt and then 1 cup of sugar, gradually, continuing to whip, until a very stiff meringue is obtained. Fold in cornstarch, followed by white vinegar.

Spoon the meringue into 5-inch round circles on the parchment paper. Use the back of a spoon to spread the meringue evenly and flatten the center, making a hollow to hold the cream and berries.

Bake for one hour or until lightly brown and quite firm. Turn the oven off and leave meringues inside with the door closed, for one more hour. Remove from the oven and set in a dry area to cool.

Meanwhile, prepare berry salad by mixing all berries together. Sprinkle with remaining 2 tablespoons sugar and toss. Chill until ready to serve.

To serve, carefully set the meringues on individual dessert plates. Top each one with whipped cream and berries. Serve immediately.

Serves 8

Blueberry Almond Cobbler

Low-fat, easy and delicious! Serve with lemon yogurt.

1 cup sorghum flour mix plus 1 tablespoon sorghum flour mix
¾ cup uncooked GF oats (or homemade granola)
¼ cup firmly packed brown sugar
¼ cup toasted almonds, chopped
¼ cup almond meal
½ teaspoon salt
½ teaspoon cinnamon
¼ teaspoon nutmeg
½ cup butter, cut-up (or stick margarine)
¼ cup granulated sugar
5 cups frozen blueberries
2 tablespoons fresh lemon juice
1 tablespoon cornstarch

Combine 1 cup sorghum flour mix, oats, brown sugar, almonds, almond meal, salt, cinnamon, and nutmeg in a large bowl. Cut in butter with a pastry blender until mixture is crumbly and begins to stick together.

Combine granulated sugar and 1 tablespoon sorghum flour mix. Toss together granulated sugar mixture, frozen blueberries, lemon juice, and cornstarch in a medium bowl. Transfer blueberry mixture to a lightly greased 2-quart baking dish. Sprinkle oat mixture evenly over blueberry mixture.

Bake 350 degrees for 50 minutes or until bubbly and golden.

Serves 8

Sour Cream Apple Cobbler

This delicious dessert will impress family or guests. Serve warm with a dollop of whipped cream, a scoop of ice cream, or by itself.
See photo on insert page G.

Dough:
1½ cups sorghum flour mix
1 teaspoon xanthan gum
1 tablespoon granulated sugar
½ teaspoon salt
½ cup butter or margarine
5 tablespoons cold water

In a mixing bowl, or food processor fitted with knife blade, combine flour, xanthan gum, sugar, and salt; mix thoroughly. Cut-in (or pulse) butter until mixture resembles coarse crumbs. Sprinkle water, 1 tablespoon at a time, until mixture holds together. Spray a 13 x 9-inch baking dish with GF baking spray. Sprinkle dough as evenly as possible in the pan. Cover with plastic wrap and press evenly to form a crust. Remove plastic wrap and refrigerate until needed.

Preheat oven to 375 degrees.

Filling:
1 cup sour cream (not light)
1 egg
1½ cups granulated sugar
1 tablespoon pure vanilla extract
1 teaspoon salt
5 large Granny Smith apples, peeled, cored, and sliced thin

Whisk sour cream and egg together in a large bowl. Add remaining dry ingredients and whisk until well blended. Add apples and stir well. Remove crust from refrigerator and pour apple filling over dough; spread evenly. Bake 45 minutes. Remove from oven and sprinkle topping evenly over apples. Bake 30 minutes more.

Topping:
1¼ cups sorghum flour mix
1 teaspoon xanthan gum
½ cup packed brown sugar
½ cup granulated sugar
1 tablespoon cinnamon
¼ teaspoon salt
1½ sticks (¾ cup) unsalted butter
Nuts, optional

In a mixing bowl, combine first six ingredients. Cut-in butter with a fork or pastry blender.

Serves 6-8

Quick Blueberry-Peach Crumble

Quinoa flakes are an excellent replacement for oats and offer wonderful nutrition. A scoop of vanilla ice cream or dollop of whipped cream completes this dessert.

1½ cups brown rice flour, divided
¾ cup packed brown sugar
1½ teaspoons ground cinnamon
¼ teaspoon ground nutmeg
Pinch of salt
½ cup quinoa flakes
10 tablespoons cold butter or margarine, cut into small pieces
2 tablespoons cornstarch
1 (16-ounce) bag frozen peaches, thawed
1 (10-ounce) bag frozen blueberries
½ cup granulated sugar
2 tablespoons lemon juice

Preheat oven to 375 degrees.

Combine 1 cup brown rice flour, brown sugar, cinnamon, nutmeg, salt, and quinoa flakes. Using pastry blender or fork, blend in butter until mixture resembles coarse crumbs. Set aside.

Toss frozen blueberries and peaches gently with cornstarch, sugar, and lemon juice. Transfer fruit to a buttered 12-inch baking dish. Spread topping evenly over fruit. Bake until topping is golden brown and fruit juices bubble, about 45 minutes.

Yield: One 12-inch cobbler

Apple Rings

Try this new variation on an apple pie and receive great compliments every time you serve it. Apple Rings require less preparation and a shorter bake time than apple pie, and this recipe can be made dairy-free.

1½ cups sorghum flour mix
½ teaspoon salt
½ cup butter, softened (use ½ cup shortening for a dairy-free version)
5-6 tablespoons iced water
3 medium Granny Smith apples, peeled, cored and shredded
½ cup granulated sugar
½ cup packed brown sugar
½ cup butter, melted (use ½ cup margarine for a dairy-free version)
½ cup water
Ground cinnamon
Whipped cream or ice cream (optional)

Preheat oven to 400 degrees.

Combine flour and salt in a mixing bowl; cut in shortening with a pastry blender until mixture resembles coarse meal. Turn mixer on low and sprinkle iced water evenly, 1 tablespoon at a time, while mixing. Mix just until dough begins to form a ball. Chill until ready to use.

Place butter, sugars, and water in a 9 x 13-inch glass baking dish. Place the baking dish in the oven until the butter is melted, about 3 minutes. Stir to dissolve the sugar, spreading mixture evenly in the pan.

Roll dough out between two sheets of plastic wrap sprayed with GF baking spray to form a 12 x 8-inch rectangle. Remove top layer of plastic wrap. Spread grated apples evenly on top of dough leaving a ½-inch margin. Lift bottom sheet of plastic wrap at the narrow end, causing the dough to roll-up, jellyroll fashion. (Use the plastic wrap to get the roll started and then use your hands to finish rolling up the dough.) Lightly score dough, making 12 marks about 1-inch apart. Slice into 12, 1-inch thick rings, placing each in the melted butter/sugar mixture. Return the pan to the oven and bake for 30 minutes. Serve warm with a dollop of whipped cream or vanilla ice cream, if desired.

Serves 6-8

Easy Low-Fat Cheesecake Squares

For crust:
8 GF chocolate sandwich crème cookies

Preheat oven to 325 degrees.

Line an 8-inch baking pan with parchment paper

Place cookies in a food processor and process into crumbs. Press into bottom of parchment lined pan.

For Filling:
1 (8-ounce) package cream cheese
1 cup sour cream
¼ cup cocoa
2 tablespoons cornstarch
¾ cup granulated sugar
1 egg white

Add cream cheese and sour cream to food processor and process until combined. Add remaining ingredients and process until smooth. Pour onto crumbs. Sprinkle chocolate chips on top. Bake 35 - 40 minutes. Cool, and then refrigerate 2 hours before serving.

Lime Squares

Tasty lime filling is combined with a graham cracker/pistachio crust for a super combination. I bake a double-batch of graham crackers and freeze one batch to use in pie crust recipes such as this one.

Crust:
4 tablespoons (½ stick) unsalted butter, melted and cooled
¾ cup shelled pistachios
1 cup GF graham cracker crumbs
¼ cup sugar

Preheat oven to 350 degrees. Spray an 8-inch square pan with GF baking spray.

In a food processor, finely grind pistachios. Add graham cracker crumbs and sugar. Add butter and pulse several times. Press into bottom of prepared pan. Bake until lightly browned, about 10 minutes. Cool crust, 15 minutes.

Filling:
2 large egg yolks
1 (14-ounce) can sweetened condensed milk
½ cup freshly squeezed lime juice

In a medium bowl, whisk together egg yolks and condensed milk. Add lime juice; whisk until smooth. Pour filling over crust, spreading to the edges. Bake until set, about 15 minutes. Cool in pan on wire rack; then chill at least one hour. Cut into 12 squares.

Yield: One dozen bars

Brownie Bites

¾ cup cocoa
1½ cups granulated sugar
2 cups sorghum flour mix
2 teaspoons xanthan gum
2 teaspoons baking powder
½ teaspoon salt
4 eggs
¾ cup canola oil
1 teaspoon pure vanilla extract
Powdered sugar

Preheat oven to 350 degrees. Spray 24 mini muffin tins with GF baking spray.

Combine cocoa, sugar, flour mix, xanthan gum, baking powder and salt in a mixing bowl, mixing well. Add eggs, canola oil, and vanilla, beating until smooth. Spoon mixture into the prepared muffin tins. Bake 10 - 13 minutes.

Cool 2 minutes, remove from pan, and cool 2 more minutes before sprinkling with powdered sugar.

Yield: 24 mini muffins

Refreshing Lime Sherbet

4 teaspoons finely grated lime rind (about 1 large lime)
1 cup granulated sugar
3 cups half and half
½ cup fresh lime juice (about 4 limes)
½ cup water
¼ teaspoon salt

Stir together first 6 ingredients in a large bowl, stirring until well blended. Pour lime mixture into freezer container of a 4-quart ice-cream maker; freeze according to manufacturer's instructions.

Makes 5 cups

Homemade Ice Cream

5 cups milk (soy milk works in this recipe for a non-dairy version)
2¼ cups granulated sugar
½ teaspoon guar gum
¼ cup plus 2 tablespoons sweet white rice flour
¼ teaspoon salt
5 eggs, beaten
4 cups half and half
1½ tablespoons pure vanilla extract

Heat milk in a 3-quart saucepan over low heat until hot but not boiling. Combine sugar, guar gum, flour, and salt; gradually add sugar mixture to milk, stirring until blended. Cook over medium heat 15 minutes or until thickened, stirring constantly. Gradually stir about one-fourth of hot mixture into beaten eggs; add to remaining hot mixture, stirring constantly. Cook 1 minute, remove from heat, and let cool. Chill at least 2 hours.

Combine half-and-half and vanilla in a large bowl; add chilled custard, stirring with a wire whisk. Pour into the freezer can of a one gallon hand-turned or electric freezer. Freeze according to manufacturer's instructions. Let ripen 1½ to 2 hours.

Yield: One gallon

Cranberry Sorbet

A wonderful, super easy sorbet to accompany your Thanksgiving or Christmas meal.

1 (16-ounce) can jellied cranberry
1 cup lemon-lime carbonated beverage

Place both ingredients in blender and blend until all bubbles are incorporated. Pour into freezable container with lid; freeze overnight.

Use fork to break-up sorbet. Scoop into serving dishes with an ice cream scoop.

Bethany's Mints

Pour these mint candies into shallow molds (found at craft stores in the cake decorating section) and serve at special occasions. Or, use a decorative mint to top a brownie or cupcake for a birthday.

1 cup granulated sugar
4 tablespoons water
1 cup powdered sugar
Peppermint extract
Food coloring

Combine granulated sugar and water in a small saucepan. Bring to a boil over medium heat. Remove from heat; add food coloring, drop of flavoring, and powdered sugar. Quickly drop on waxed paper or fill candy molds. Return pot to the warm burner, stirring constantly, if mixture hardens too quickly.

Cookies
and
Bars

Easy Oat-Almond Crisps

Great as a cookie, snack, or breakfast!

¼ cup packed brown sugar
¼ cup (½ stick) salted butter, melted
1 large egg
½ teaspoon pure vanilla extract
1½ cups GF oats
½ cup sliced almonds

Preheat oven to 350 degrees.

Combine all ingredients in a mixing bowl; mix well with spoon. Drop dough onto parchment lined sheet, making 12 cookies. Flatten each with the back of the spoon. Bake until golden, about 15 minutes. Cool completely on baking sheet.

Yield: One dozen

Delicate Crispy Almond Cookies

This recipe boasts of having no butter, shortening, or margarine, making it a tasty treat without the fat of most cookies. Be sure to measure the ingredients accurately. See photo on insert page G.

¾ cup almond meal (almonds processed in a food processor work fine)
¾ cup sorghum flour (not mix)
1½ cups powdered sugar
6 tablespoons plus 1 teaspoon olive oil
7 teaspoons water

Preheat oven to 350 degrees. Line an 11 x 17-inch cookie sheet with parchment paper.

Combine all ingredients in a mixing bowl; mix well with a spoon. (Note: Do not let dough "sit" as it will dry-out. Do not freeze or refrigerate dough.) Drop dough, by the teaspoon, onto parchment-lined cookie sheets, 12 cookies per pan. Bake 12 minutes. Cool completely before removing cookies from pan.

Yield: About 30 cookies

Spritz Cookies

Spritz cookies are a Christmas tradition in our family.
See photo on insert page D.

1 cup softened salted butter
¾ cup granulated sugar
1 egg
1 teaspoon pure vanilla extract
2¼ cups sorghum flour mix
2 teaspoons xanthan gum
¼ teaspoon baking powder

Preheat oven to 375 degrees.

Cream the butter and sugar in a large mixing bowl. Beat in egg and vanilla. Sift dry ingredients into a separate bowl. Gradually add dry ingredients to butter/sugar mixture, forming a soft dough. Refrigerate dough at least one hour.

Fill cookie press with cold dough and form cookies on an ungreased, high quality cookie sheet. Sprinkle with your favorite GF jimmies or colored sugar.

Bake 10 minutes or until lightly browned. Cool cookies 3 minutes on the baking sheet then transfer to a rack to finish cooling.

Note: For a non-dairy version use 1 cup Fleishmann's unsalted sticks plus ½ teaspoon salt.

Yield: Two dozen cookies

Flourless Peanut-Butter Oatmeal Cookies

¼ cup butter, softened
¼ cup granulated sugar
1 cup packed brown sugar
2 eggs
1 teaspoon pure vanilla extract
1 cup GF peanut butter
1¼ teaspoons baking soda
3 cups GF oats
¾ cup GF semi-sweet chocolate chips

Preheat oven to 350 degrees. Spray a cookie sheet with GF baking spray.

Cream butter and sugars in a large mixing bowl. Add eggs, vanilla, and peanut butter; cream for 2 minutes more. Add remaining ingredients and mix until combined. Drop by large teaspoonfuls onto prepared cookie sheet. Bake 10 - 13 minutes.

Yield: 18-24 cookies

Variation:
Replace chocolate chips with ¾ cup GF butterscotch chips or ¾ cup candy-coated chocolate pieces

Peanut Butter Cookies

*These flourless cookies are a snap to make,
requiring only three ingredients.*

1 cup granulated sugar
1 egg
1 cup GF peanut butter

Preheat oven to 350 degrees. Spray cookie sheet with GF baking spray. Combine all ingredients in mixing bowl, mixing well. Drop by heaping teaspoonfuls onto prepared cookie sheet. Bake 12-15 minutes.

Yield: Two dozen cookies

Chunky Peanut Butter Chocolate-Chip Cookies

1 stick (½ cup) unsalted butter, softened
½ cup GF peanut butter
½ cup packed brown sugar
¼ cup granulated sugar
2 eggs
½ teaspoon pure vanilla extract
1½ cups sorghum flour mix
¼ teaspoon baking soda
½ teaspoon baking powder
1 teaspoon xanthan gum
½ cup roasted peanuts, coarsely chopped
1 cup semi-sweet or bittersweet chocolate chips
Fleur de sel (optional)

Preheat oven to 350 degrees.

In a large mixing bowl, cream the butter, peanut butter, brown sugar, sugar, egg, and vanilla extract. Sift together flour, baking soda, baking powder, and xanthan gum. Combine dry ingredients with the peanut butter mixture, stirring well. Stir in the chopped peanuts and chocolate chips.

Drop generous spoonfuls of dough onto an ungreased cookie sheet. Press each mound of dough with a fork to flatten slightly.

Bake until bottom of cookies are golden brown, about 10 minutes. Remove from oven and sprinkle immediately with fleur de sel to taste. Let cookies cool on the cookie sheet for a few minutes before transferring to a cooling rack to cool completely.

Chocolate-Chip Macaroons

Super-easy, melt-in-your-mouth cookies are only minutes away!

1 (14-ounce) can GF sweetened condensed milk
2¾ cup dried flaked coconut
¼ to ½ teaspoon pure almond extract
¼ teaspoon salt
1½ cups chocolate chips

Preheat oven to 350 degrees.

Combine all ingredients in a mixing bowl; mix well. Drop cookies by the tablespoon onto a cookie sheet sprayed with GF baking spray. Bake 12 minutes or until edges are lightly browned.

Yield: Two dozen

Chocolate-Chip Cookies

Freeze this cookie dough in portions for warm cookies anytime.

1 cup softened salted butter or margarine
¼ cup granulated sugar
¾ cup light brown sugar
1 teaspoon pure vanilla extract
1 (3.9-ounce) package GF vanilla instant pudding
2 eggs
1½ cup sorghum flour mix
1 teaspoon baking soda
½ teaspoon xanthan gum
2 cups of chocolate chips

Preheat oven to 325 degrees.

Combine butter, sugars, vanilla, and pudding, in a mixing bowl; cream until smooth. Beat in eggs. Gradually add flour, baking soda, and xanthan gum; blend until smooth. Stir in chocolate chips. Drop by teaspoonfuls onto ungreased high quality cookie sheets. Bake 8 minutes. Cool cookies 3 minutes before transferring to a wire rack.

Yield: Two dozen

No-Egg
Chocolate-Chip Cookies

These cookies, with their crisp exterior and soft interior, are favorites with my kids. Margarine and dairy-free chocolate chips will offer a dairy-free version.

1 stick (½ cup) butter or margarine
½ cup shortening
¼ cup almond butter
¾ teaspoon baking soda in 1 tablespoon water
½ teaspoon salt
¾ cup packed brown sugar
¼ cup granulated sugar
1 teaspoon pure vanilla extract
1¾ cups sorghum flour
¾ cup tapioca flour
1½ cup chocolate chips

Preheat oven to 350 degrees. Generously spray a good quality baking sheet with GF baking spray.

In a large mixing bowl combine the butter or margarine, shortening, and almond butter until smooth. Add baking soda, salt, sugars, and vanilla; mixing well. Add flours and chocolate chips, mixing until combined.

Drop cookies by heaping tablespoons onto prepared cookie sheet. Bake 11-13 minutes. Cool on cookie sheet 3 minutes then remove from pan to finish cooling.

Yield: 24 large cookies
22 minutes or until tester comes out clean.

Yield: 6 mini loaves

Soft Chocolate-Chip Cookies

These chocolate chip cookies use less sugar than most cookie recipes and do not dry out as quickly as other GF homemade cookies.

1¼ cups sorghum flour mix
¾ teaspoon salt
¼ teaspoon baking soda
½ teaspoon xanthan gum
7 tablespoons unsalted butter, or GF unsalted margarine
¼ cup granulated sugar
¼ cup packed brown sugar
1 large egg
1 teaspoon pure vanilla extract
3 tablespoons sour cream or GF plain yogurt
1¼ cups semisweet chocolate chips

Preheat oven to 350 degrees. Spray a cookie sheet with GF baking spray.

Whisk together flour, salt, baking soda, and xanthan gum in a medium bowl; set aside.

Beat butter and sugars with a mixer on medium speed until pale and fluffy, 3 - 5 minutes. Beat in egg and vanilla. Reduce speed to low. Add flour mixture in 2 batches, alternating with sour cream; beat until just combined. Stir in chocolate chips. Cover and freeze 10 minutes.

Drop cookies by the tablespoon onto the prepared baking sheet, spacing 2 inches apart. Bake until centers are set and cookies are pale golden brown, 12 - 14 minutes.

Yield: Two dozen cookies

Chocolate Meringue Cookies

Crisp on the outside, airy and chewy on the inside, these flourless cookies can be made in a snap. See photo on insert page B

2 large egg whites
¼ teaspoon cream of tartar
¾ cup granulated sugar
1 teaspoon pure vanilla extract
1 cup chocolate chips
¼ cup chopped pecans

Preheat oven to 275 degrees; line a cookie sheet with parchment paper.

Place chocolate chips in a microwavable bowl and heat in a microwave for 3 minutes at low to medium power until chips are almost melted. Stir until completely melted; set aside.

In a large mixing bowl, whip egg whites until foamy. Add cream of tartar and beat until soft peaks form. Add sugar gradually, whipping until stiff but not dry. Beat in vanilla. Fold in chocolate and nuts.

Drop onto paper-lined cookie sheet, dividing dough into 12 cookies. Bake 25 minutes. Allow to completely cool before removing from pan.

Yield: One dozen cookies

Soft Cinnamon-Sugar Cookies

¼ cup canola oil
2 eggs
1 teaspoon pure vanilla extract
1½ teaspoons cinnamon
½ cup navy bean flour
½ cup sorghum flour mix
½ cup granulated sugar
¼ teaspoon salt
½ teaspoon baking soda
½ teaspoon xanthan gum

Preheat oven to 350 degrees. Spray a good quality baking sheet with GF baking spray.

Combine the oil, eggs, and vanilla in a large bowl. Stir the dry ingredients together in a medium bowl, and then add them to the wet ingredients, stirring well.

Drop dough by tablespoonfuls onto prepared cookie sheet. Sprinkle the top with sugar if you want a crisper, crinkled cookie. Bake 12 minutes. Cool on the baking sheet for 2 minutes before removing from pan.

Yield: 1½ dozen

Roll-Out Sugar Cookies

An adaptation of my grandmother's recipe, these sugar cookies roll-out easily and hold together well.

1¼ cups fine white rice flour
½ cup sorghum flour mix
¼ cup tapioca starch flour
¼ cup plus 1 tablespoon potato starch
1 cup granulated sugar
¾ cup shortening
1 teaspoon pure vanilla extract
1 egg
4 teaspoons water
1½ teaspoons baking powder
½ teaspoon salt
1 teaspoon xanthan gum

Preheat oven to 375 degrees.

Line cookie sheets with parchment paper, or spray good quality cookie sheets with GF baking spray.

Cream shortening and sugar in a large mixing bowl. Add egg, mixing until combined. Add remaining ingredients and mix well.

Roll-out half of dough on board sprinkled with tapioca flour. Cut cookies with cookie cutters, returning extra dough to the mixing bowl. Place cut cookies on the prepared cookie sheet. Sprinkle cookies with colored sugar. Bake 8-9 minutes.

Sprinkle board with tapioca flour and repeat above steps with second half of dough.

Yield: Two dozen cookies

No-Bake Cereal Cookies

These easy cookies are nut-free thanks to new spreads made from sunflower seeds.

½ cup sugar
¾ cup brown rice syrup
1 teaspoon pure vanilla extract
1 cup sunflower seed butter (I used Sunbutter)
2 cups Perky's Nutty Rice cereal
1 cup Perky's O's cereal
¼ cup sorghum flour mix
½ teaspoon xanthan gum
4 teaspoons tapioca flour
1 teaspoon cinnamon

Heat sugar and brown rice syrup in a small saucepan over medium- high heat until sugar is dissolved and syrup is thin.

Meanwhile, combine remaining ingredients in a mixing bowl and mix well. Add sugar/syrup mixture and mix well. Form into balls and allow cookies to cool. Store in an airtight container.

Yield: Two dozen cookies

Nut Balls

Substitute your favorite nuts, seeds, and dried fruit to create endless variations for this nutritious "trail-mix-rolled-into-a-ball." Super yummy and super easy…no mixing or baking required! See photo on insert page D.

½ cup pecans
¾ cup almonds
¾ cup dried cranberries
½ cup dried apricots
½ cup pumpkin seeds
¼ cup sunflower seeds
Dash of salt (only if seeds and nuts are unsalted)
¼ cup orange juice concentrate
Granulated sugar, powdered sugar, or dried flaked coconut

Place first seven ingredients in the bowl of a food processor. Pulse until nuts and fruit are well-chopped. Add orange juice concentrate; pulse until mixture holds together. Add more concentrate, by the tablespoon, if necessary. Form into small balls and roll in sugar or coconut. Refrigerate in an airtight container.

Energy Bites

1 cup sunflower seeds
2 cups dried flaked coconut
½ cup milled flaxseed (also called flaxseed meal)
1 egg plus 1 egg white
½ cup honey
½ cup semi-sweet mini chocolate chips
¼ teaspoon salt (omit if sunflower seeds are salted)

Preheat oven to 375 degrees. Spray 24 mini muffin tins with GF baking spray.

In a food processor fitted knife blade, ground sunflower seeds to a flourlike consistency. Combine ground sunflower seeds with remaining ingredients; mixing well. Fill mini muffin tins to the top; pack down with the back of a spoon. Bake 10 minutes. Allow to cool completely before removing from pan.

Makes two dozen mini muffin bites

Orange-Almond Biscotti

½ stick unsalted butter (4 tablespoons), melted
1 tablespoon fine dried orange rind
1 cup sorghum flour mix
¼ cup yellow cornmeal
½ cup granulated sugar
½ teaspoon xanthan gum
1 teaspoon baking soda
¼ teaspoon salt
3 large eggs
½ teaspoon pure vanilla extract
¾ cup chopped toasted almonds

Preheat oven to 350 degrees. Line a baking sheet with parchment paper.

Pour melted butter in a large mixing bowl. Add orange rind and next eight ingredients. Using paddle attachment, beat at high speed until fluffy, about 2 minutes. Stir in chopped almonds. Form dough into 6 mounds on prepared baking sheet.

Bake, rotating sheet once, until golden brown, about 22-25 minutes. Reduce temperature to 200 degrees. Remove pan from oven and, using a serrated knife, cut mounds on the diagonal into ½-inch-thick slices. Arrange slices in a single layer on the parchment-lined baking sheet and return to the oven to bake until dry and crisp, about 30 minutes.

Store in an airtight container at room temperature for up to two weeks, or in the freezer for up to 3 months.

Yield: Two dozen cookies

Egg Free Biscotti
In a small bowl add 6 tablespoons water to ½ cup flaxseed meal, stirring well; set aside. Follow directions above, substituting almond meal for the cornmeal, flaxseed mixture for the eggs, and pure almond extract for the vanilla extract.

Slice-n-Bake
Coconut Tea Cookies

See photo on insert page E.

½ cup sorghum flour mix or fine white rice flour (not mix)
½ teaspoon baking powder
¼ teaspoon salt
¼ cup (½ stick) butter
½ cup granulated sugar
1 large egg
½ teaspoon pure vanilla extract
1½ cups unsweetened dried flaked coconut
Powdered sugar for dusting

Whisk flour, baking powder, and salt in a medium bowl.

Combine butter and sugar in a large mixing bowl. Mix on medium-high speed until pale and fluffy, about 2 minutes. Mix in the egg and vanilla. Reduce speed to low; gradually mix in flour mixture. Stir in coconut.

On a sheet of plastic wrap, shape dough into a log about 1 to 1¼- inch in diameter. Wrap the plastic wrap completely around the log. Refrigerate until cold, about 30 minutes.

Preheat oven to 375 degrees. Spray a baking sheet with GF baking spray.

Remove plastic wrap from cookies and slice cookies about ½-inch thick, placing them on the prepared baking sheet. Bake until tops turn golden, about 8 - 10 minutes. Let cookies cool completely on baking sheets placed on wire racks. Dust with powdered sugar if desired.

Yield: 24 cookies

Animal Grahams

*These small crisp cookies are a reminder of some we enjoyed before Celiac Disease. They can be rolled-out and cut into shapes,
or form the dough into small balls and press twice, in criss-cross fashion with a fork dipped in a cinnamon-sugar mixture.
The thinner you press the cookies, the crisper they will be.*

½ cup margarine
¼ cup honey
1 cup packed brown sugar
1 teaspoon pure vanilla extract
1¾ cups sorghum flour (or 1½ cups sorghum flour plus ¼ cup amaranth
    flour)
1 cup tapioca flour
¼ cup cornstarch
1 teaspoon xanthan gum
1 teaspoon salt
2 teaspoons cinnamon
2 teaspoons baking powder
About ½ cup water

Cream margarine, honey, brown sugar, and vanilla. Combine dry ingredients in a separate bowl. Stir dry ingredients into creamed mixture, alternating with water. Add more water if necessary, by the tablespoon, until dough holds together and forms a ball.

For drop cookies:
Form cookies into small balls and place on cookie sheet sprayed with GF baking spray or parchment-lined cookie sheet. Press balls flat with fork dipped in sugar/cinnamon mixture. Bake at 375 degrees for 12 - 14 minutes. Cool slightly before removing from pan. Store cooled cookies in an airtight container.

For graham crackers:
Divide dough between two 11 x 17-inch jellyroll pans which have been sprayed with GF baking spray. Spray a sheet of plastic wrap with GF baking spray and place plastic on dough, sprayed-side down. Roll with a non-rimmed drinking glass turned on its side until dough is evenly spread to edges of each pan (about ¼ inch thick). Sprinkle with cinnamon and sugar if desired. Prick dough all over with fork. Bake at 375 degrees for 13 - 15 minutes (or longer, depending on thickness). Score graham crackers in the pan while still warm, then remove graham crackers from the pan to finish cooling. Store in an airtight container. All cookies freeze well.

Brownies

My previous book did not include brownies because I had not come up with a recipe that equaled the store-bought mixes. This recipe however, is fabulous; especially considering it is free of wheat, dairy, soy, eggs, refined sugar, and nuts!

1 cup sorghum flour mix
¼ cup cornstarch
2¼ teaspoons baking powder
¼ teaspoons baking soda
¼ teaspoons xanthan gum
1 teaspoons salt
½ cup cocoa
½ cup unsweetened applesauce
¾ cup honey (or 10 tablespoons plus 2 teaspoons agave nectar)
½ cup canola oil
2 tablespoons pure vanilla extract
½ cup hot water
2 cups dairy-free, GF chocolate chips

Preheat oven to 325 degrees.

Spray 3 dozen mini-muffin tins or 24 regular-size muffin tins with GF cooking spray.

In a medium bowl, whisk together flour, cornstarch, baking powder, baking soda, xanthan gum, salt, and unsweetened cocoa; set aside.

In a large bowl, mix together applesauce, honey, canola oil, and vanilla. Slowly add to flour mixture, stirring to combine. Stir in hot water until it forms a batter. Fold in chocolate chips.

Place 1 tablespoon batter into each prepared muffin cup. Transfer muffin pans to oven, and bake until a toothpick inserted in center of a muffin comes out clean, about 12 - 14 minutes for mini-muffins, or 16 minutes for regular size muffins. Let cool before unmolding.

Yield: 3 dozen mini muffins or 24 regular size muffins

Granola Bar Variations

Granola Bars were such a popular item from my first cookbook that I came up with three variations. Granola Bars are easy to make, freeze well, and are a healthy breakfast, lunchbox food, or snack. Send the bars, straight from the freezer, to school, for travel, or as an on-the-go snack. Come up with your own variations substituting seeds, nuts, and dried fruit of your choice. Pictured on insert page E.

Craisins, Coconut, and O's Granola Bars

1 cup packed brown sugar
¾ cup almond butter
½ cup honey
½ cup margarine, melted
2 teaspoons pure vanilla extract
3 cups organic oats
1 cup shredded coconut
1½ cups O's cereal (I use Perky O's original)
½ cup chopped craisins

Gingersnap Granola Bars

1 cup packed brown sugar
¾ cup almond butter
¼ cup honey
¼ cup blackstrap molasses
2 teaspoons pure vanilla extract
3 cups organic oat bran
½ cup raisins
1 teaspoon cinnamon
1 teaspoon ginger
½ teaspoon cloves
¼ teaspoon cardamom
½ teaspoon salt
1 cup organic oats

Pecan, Coconut, and Chocolate Chip Granola Bars

1 cup packed brown sugar
¾ cup almond butter
½ cup honey
½ cup margarine, melted
2 teaspoons pure vanilla extract
¾ cup coarsely chopped pecans
¾ cup semi-sweet chocolate chips
1 cup coconut
½ cup flaxseed meal
3 cups organic oats

For all variations: Preheat oven to 350 degrees. Spray an 11 x 17-inch pan with GF baking spray. Combine all ingredients in a large mixing bowl and mix well. Spread evenly into the prepared pan. Bake 17-20 minutes (or longer if you want them crisper). Cut into bars while still warm, then allow bars to completely cool in the pan. Store in an airtight tin.

Lemon Bars

¼ cup powdered sugar
½ cup butter, softened
1 cup sorghum flour mix
Pinch of salt
2 eggs
1 cup granulated sugar
2 tablespoons fresh lemon juice
1 tablespoon cornstarch

Preheat oven to 350 degrees.

For the crust, cream sugar and butter until fluffy. Add flour and salt, mixing until combined. Press into a 9 x 9-inch baking pan sprayed with GF baking spray. Bake 10 minutes.

For the filling, combine the eggs, sugar, lemon juice, and cornstarch, mixing well. Pour over the baked, cooled crust. Bake 350 degrees for 20 minutes.

Yield: 12 lemon bars

Rocky Road Bars

8 tablespoons unsalted butter or margarine
½ cup unsweetened cocoa powder
1 cup packed brown sugar
1 large egg
½ cup sorghum flour mix
½ teaspoon xanthan gum
½ cup milk
1 teaspoon pure vanilla extract
1 cup mini marshmallows
1 cup coarsely chopped walnuts or pecans
1 cup semisweet chocolate chips

Preheat oven to 350 degrees. Spray an 8-inch square pan with GF baking spray.

Place butter and cocoa in a medium saucepan over low heat, stirring until butter is melted and mixture is smooth. Remove from heat. Stir in brown sugar, egg, flour mix, xanthan gum, milk, and vanilla.

Spread mixture evenly in the prepared pan. Bake until a toothpick inserted in center comes out clean, about 30 minutes. Remove pan from oven and immediately top with marshmallows, nuts, and chocolate chips. Cover lightly with foil to trap heat, causing marshmallows and chips to "halfway" melt.

Makes one 8-inch pan

Fudgy Cookie Bars

1½ cups sorghum flour mix
¾ cup powdered sugar
½ cup unsweetened cocoa
1 cup salted butter, cut into pieces
1 (14-ounce) can sweetened condensed milk
1 teaspoon pure vanilla extract
2 cups semisweet chocolate morsels
1 cup chopped pecans or morsels
Dried flaked coconut

Preheat oven to 350 degrees. Spray a 13 x 9-inch baking pan with baking spray.

Combine first three ingredients in a large bowl; cut in cold butter pieces with a pastry blender or fork until crumbly. Press mixture into the bottom of the prepared pan. Bake for 15 minutes. Cool on a wire rack.

Stir together milk, vanilla, and 1 cup of chocolate chips in a small saucepan over medium heat, stirring occasionally, 5 minutes or until melted and smooth. Pour mixture evenly over prepared crust, spreading evenly to the edges of the pan. Sprinkle with chopped pecans or walnuts, remaining chocolate morsels, and coconut; press down slightly. Bake 25 minutes.

Makes 24 bars

Jam Bars Revisited

*Almond extract added to the dough,
and a splash of fresh lemon juice added to the raspberry filling,
make this favorite recipe from my first book, even better.*

1½ cups sorghum flour mix
½ cup brown sugar
1 teaspoon xanthan gum
1½ teaspoons baking powder
½ teaspoon salt
½ teaspoon pure almond extract
1 cup (2 sticks) butter or margarine
1½ cups oats
½ cup flaked coconut
½ cup chopped pecans
1 (17-ounce) jar raspberry jam
1 teaspoon fresh lemon juice

Preheat oven to 350 degrees.

Spray a 9 x 13-inch pan with GF baking spray.

Mix flour, brown sugar, xanthan gum, baking powder, and salt in a large bowl. Sprinkle almond extract over dry ingredients. Cut in butter or margarine until mixture resembles coarse meal. Add oats, coconut, and pecans; mix well.

Reserve two cups (not packed) of the crumb mixture in a small bowl. Press remaining crumb mixture firmly into the bottom of the pan. Combine jam and lemon juice. Spoon evenly over top; sprinkle with reserved crumb mixture.

Bake 25 - 30 minutes. Cool completely. Cut into bars. Serve at room temperature or chilled.

Makes 24 bars

Cakes

Chocolate Truffle Cheesecake

Smooth, creamy, and wonderfully rich tasting, this cheesecake will fool anyone. Slice it into 16 servings and this recipe boasts 36g carbohydrates, 10g fat, 25g sugars, and 275k cal per slice!.

For the crust:
1 cup GF chocolate cookie crumbs
1 tablespoon packed brown sugar
1 tablespoon canola oil
1 teaspoon instant coffee granules dissolved in 2 teaspoons hot
  water

Blend crumbs, sugar, oil and coffee in small bowl with a fork or your fingertips. Press into the bottom of a 9-inch spring form pan sprayed with cooking spray.

Preheat oven to 325 degrees.

For the cheesecake:
24-ounces low fat (1%) cottage cheese
12-ounces cream cheese (may use reduced fat if it is GF)
1 cup packed brown sugar
½ cup granulated sugar
¾ cup unsweetened cocoa powder
¼ cup cornstarch
1 large egg
2 large egg whites
1 teaspoon instant coffee dissolved in 1 teaspoon boiling water
2 teaspoons GF pure vanilla extract
¼ teaspoon salt
1-ounce semi-sweet baking chocolate, melted
1-ounce unsweetened baking chocolate, melted

Bring water to a boil for the water bath.

Puree cottage cheese in a food processor until very smooth, stopping to scrape down sides. Add cream cheese, brown sugar, granulated sugar, cocoa, and cornstarch; process until smooth. Add egg, egg whites, coffee, vanilla, salt, and chocolate, blending well. Pour into the crust lined pan.

Place the cheesecake on a piece of heavy-duty foil and wrap foil upward. Place foil-protected pan in a roasting pan or skillet. Pour enough boiling water into the skillet or pan to come 1-inch up the side of the spring form pan.

Bake the cheesecake until the edges are set but the center still jiggles, about 50 minutes. Turn off the oven. Let the cheesecake stand in the oven, with the door ajar, for 1 hour. Transfer the cheesecake from the water bath to a wire rack; remove foil. Cool to room temperature, about 2 hours. Refrigerate, uncovered, until chilled.

Yield: 16 servings

Cream Filled Cupcakes

These cupcakes are pictured on insert page D.

Prepare Old Fashioned Chocolate Cake page 101. Generously spray 24 muffin cups with GF baking spray. Fill each ½ full with batter. Bake 15-18 minutes or until tester comes out clean. Remove from pan after 5 minutes. Prepare cream filling below.

Cream Filling:
¼ cup butter
¼ cup shortening
2 cups confectioners' sugar
1 pinch salt
3 tablespoons milk
1 teaspoon pure vanilla extract

In a large bowl beat butter and shortening together until smooth. Blend in confectioners' sugar and salt. Gradually beat in 3 tablespoons milk and 1 teaspoon vanilla; beat until light and fluffy. Fill a pastry bag with a small tip. Push tip through bottom of cupcake and fill each cupcake. Place inverted cupcakes on a serving platter. Prepare frosting, adding milk by the tablespoon until frosting can be drizzled. Drizzle frosting over each cupcake.

Frosting:
¼ cup cocoa
¾ cup powdered sugar
2 tablespoons milk

Deep Dish Apple Cake

5 peeled, cored, sliced Granny Smith apples
1¼ cup granulated sugar plus 4 tablespoons granulated sugar
2 teaspoons cinnamon, divided
1 cup sorghum flour mix
1 cup canola oil
2 teaspoons pure vanilla extract
½ teaspoon salt
¼ cup orange juice
3 eggs

Spray a 2-inch deep, 8 x 12-inch pan with GF cooking spray. Preheat oven to 350 degrees.

Mix apples, 4 tablespoons sugar, and 1 teaspoon cinnamon in a large bowl, stir well; set aside.

Combine remaining 1 teaspoon cinnamon, sorghum flour mix, canola oil, 1¼ cup sugar, vanilla extract, salt, orange juice, and eggs in a large mixing bowl. Beat on low speed 3 minutes.   Scrape half of batter into pan. Top with apple mixture. Scrape remaining batter over apples. Sprinkle topping evenly over batter. Bake 1 hour.

Topping:
½ cup sorghum flour mix
4 tablespoon butter, softened
1 teaspoon cinnamon
¼ cup granulated sugar

Combine all in a medium bowl and mix with a pastry blender or fork until crumbly.

Light Upside-Down Apple Cake

This low-fat cake offers the benefit of omega-3's from flaxseed. I make this cake in a 10-inch cast iron skillet but a 9 or 10-inch cake pan will work as well.

1 tablespoon corn syrup
1 tablespoon butter
¾ cup packed brown sugar, divided
3 tablespoons chopped pecans
3 medium size Brae burn apples, peeled, cored, and sliced
¾ cup sorghum flour mix
½ cup flaxseed meal
1 teaspoon baking powder
¼ teaspoon salt
2 teaspoons dried grated orange rind
1 teaspoon pure vanilla extract
2 large eggs
2 large egg whites
¼ cup granulated sugar
½ cup whipping cream (optional)

Preheat oven to 375 degrees.

Melt corn syrup and butter in a 10-inch cast iron skillet over medium heat. Remove from heat. Sprinkle with ½ cup brown sugar and pecans. Arrange apple slices over brown sugar mixture.

Combine flour, flaxseed meal, baking powder, and salt in a large bowl, stirring well. In a medium bowl, combine remaining ¼ cup brown sugar, rind, vanilla, and 2 eggs, stirring with a whisk. Beat egg whites with a mixer at high speed until soft peaks form. Add ¼ cup granulated sugar, 1 tablespoon at a time, beating until stiff peaks form. Add whole egg mixture to flour mixture; stir just until moist. Gently fold in egg white mixture. Spoon batter over apples.

Bake 25 - 27 minutes or until knife inserted in center comes out clean. Cool in pan 5 minutes. Loosen sides of cake with knife; place a plate over skillet and invert cake onto the plate. Cut into wedges and serve with whipping cream if desired.

Yield: 8 servings

Moist White Cake

The best gluten-free white cake I have tasted, Moist White Cake is great topped with berries and cream, frosted for a birthday cake, or sprinkled with powdered sugar. And, this cake is still moist the second day.

1½ cups sorghum flour
½ cup white rice flour
¼ cup tapioca flour
¼ cup sweet white rice flour
¼ cup cornstarch
1¾ cups granulated sugar
2 teaspoons baking powder
1½ teaspoons baking soda
½ teaspoon salt
1 teaspoon xanthan gum
2 eggs
1 cup plain yogurt
½ cup canola oil
2 teaspoons pure vanilla extract
1 cup boiling water

Preheat oven to 350 degrees.

Generously spray a 13 x 9-inch baking pan, or three 8-inch round baking pans with GF baking spray.

Combine the first 10 ingredients in a large mixing bowl. Add eggs, yogurt, oil, and vanilla. Mix on low speed until combined, then beat on high speed for 3 minutes. Stir in boiling water. Pour into the prepared pan.

Bake 28 -32 minutes or until tester comes out clean, or about 18 minutes for three 8-inch pans.

Cool in pan or invert after 5 minutes then frost as desired.

Yield: One 13 x 9-inch sheet cake, or one 8-inch round layered cake

Strawberry Cake Variation:
Reduce pure vanilla extract to ½ teaspoon and add 1 teaspoon strawberry flavoring. Add several drops of red food coloring until batter is desired shade of pink.

Old-Fashioned
Chocolate Cake

Don't tell, and they'll never know that this cake is gluten-free!
Frosted, it will stay moist for two days.

2 cups sugar
1¾ cups sorghum flour mix
1 cup cocoa
2 teaspoons baking powder
1½ teaspoons baking soda
½ teaspoon salt
1 teaspoon xanthan gum
2 eggs
1 cup plain GF yogurt
½ cup canola oil
2 teaspoons pure vanilla extract
1 cup boiling water

Preheat oven to 350 degrees. Prepare one 13 x 9-inch pan or two 9-inch round pans by spraying with GF baking spray.

Mix dry ingredients in a large mixing bowl. Add all wet ingredients except water. Beat on high 2 minutes. Stir in boiling water with a rubber spatula, scraping the sides and bottom of the bowl. Pour batter into prepared pan.

Bake 30 minutes or until a tester comes out clean. Do not over bake. Allow 13 x 9-inch pan to cool completely before frosting. Allow round pans to cool for 15 minutes before inverting; cool completely before frosting.

Yield: One 13 x 9-inch sheet cake or, one 9-inch round layer cake

Chocolate Pound Cake

This cake travels well and keeps well for several days.
Or, serve it warm from the oven with a scoop of vanilla ice cream and
hot fudge topping for a special treat!

2 cups sorghum flour mix
½ cup unsweetened cocoa
1 cup sour cream
½ cup granulated sugar
½ cup packed brown sugar
1 box (3.9-ounce) instant chocolate pudding
3 eggs
¾ cup water
¼ cup canola oil
1 tablespoon baking powder
2 cups semisweet chocolate chips

Preheat oven to 350 degrees. Spray a Bundt pan with GF baking spray.

Combine all ingredients in a mixing bowl. Beat at high speed for 2 minutes, stopping to scrape sides of bowl and beater.

Scrape batter into the prepared pan. Bake 35 minutes or until tester comes out clean.

Serves 12

Hot Fudge Molten Cakes

Molten cakes ooze with a warm filling, in this case, chocolate fudge!
These small cakes are a big hit for just about any special occasion.

½ cup butter
¼ cup sorghum flour mix
6 ounces semisweet good quality baking chocolate, chopped
3 tablespoons GF hot fudge topping
½ cup granulated sugar
3 large eggs, at room temperature
Pinch of salt
Vanilla ice cream
Nuts such as pecans or walnuts

Preheat the oven to 425 degrees. Spray four, 6-ounce ramekins generously with GF baking spray. Transfer the ramekins to a sturdy baking sheet.

In a small bowl, blend the hot fudge topping with 1 tablespoon powdered sugar; set aside.

Melt the chocolate with the butter in the microwave until melted; set aside to cool.

Add granulated sugar, eggs, and salt to a mixing bowl and beat until thick and pale yellow, about 3 minutes. Using a rubber spatula, fold in the melted chocolate until well combined. Fold in ¼ cup of the flour mix. Divide two thirds of the batter among the four prepared ramekins. Spoon fudge mixture onto the center of each. Cover with remaining batter. Bake in the center of the oven for 16 minutes, until the tops are cracked but the centers are still slightly jiggly. Transfer the ramekins to a rack and let cool for 2 minutes. Run the tip of a small knife around each cake to loosen. Invert a small plate over each cake and, using pot holders, invert the cake onto the plate. Carefully lift off the ramekin. Top each cake with a scoop of vanilla ice cream and/or nuts; serve immediately.

Makes 4 individual cakes

Mississippi Mud Molten Cakes
Make as directed but substitute one large marshmallow for the hot fudge topping. Drizzle the top of inverted warm cakes with chocolate, then top with nuts.

Lemon Birthday Cake

My daughter loves all things "lemon." This was her 13th birthday cake and was quite well received by even those who are not so crazy about lemon.

For cake:
3 cups sorghum flour (not mix)
½ cup tapioca starch flour
½ cup potato starch
½ teaspoon salt
1 tablespoon baking powder
1 teaspoon xanthan gum
1 cup milk
1 cup canola oil
1 teaspoon pure vanilla extract
1 tablespoon finely grated lemon zest
2 cups granulated sugar
3 large eggs

For lemon curd:
¼ cup fresh lemon juice
¼ cup plus 2 tablespoons granulated sugar
3 large egg yolks
¼ teaspoon guar gum
½ stick unsalted butter, cut into pieces
¼ teaspoon lemon extract

For lemon frosting:
2 sticks unsalted butter, softened
3½ cups powdered sugar
¼ cup fresh lemon juice
12 teaspoons lemon extract
2 teaspoons finely grated lemon zest

Preheat oven to 350 degrees.

Generously spray two 9-inch round cake pans with GF baking spray.

Whisk together sorghum flour, potato starch, and tapioca starch, salt, baking powder, and xanthan gum until combined.

Stir together milk, canola oil, vanilla, and zest in a separate bowl.

Beat together sugar and eggs in a large bowl with an electric mixer at medium speed just until combined, about 1 minute. Reduce speed to low and add flour mixture alternately with milk mixture, mixing just until combined.

Divide batter evenly between cake pans, smoothing tops, and bake until a tester comes out clean, 35 - 40 minutes.

Cool cake layers in pans on racks 5 minutes. Invert onto cooling racks.

For Curd:
Whisk together zest, lemon juice, sugar, yolks, a pinch of salt, and guar gum in a 1-quart heavy saucepan. Add butter and cook over moderately low heat, whisking constantly, until curd is thick enough to hold marks of the whisk and first bubbles appear on surface, about 5 minutes. Whisk in extract. Immediately pour curd into a bowl, then cover surface with wax paper and chill until cold, about 30 minutes.

For Frosting:
Beat butter with an electric mixer at high speed until light and fluffy, about 1 minute. Reduce speed to low and add powdered sugar, lemon juice, extract, and zest, mixing until creamy and smooth, about 2 minutes.

To frost cake, halve each layer with a long serrated knife. Spread bottom half of each layer with lemon curd, then top with remaining cake layers to form two sandwiched layers. Place first sandwiched layer on cake stand and spread frosting on top. Place second sandwiched layer on top of first layer and frost top and sides of cake with remaining frosting.

Makes one, 9-inch layer cake

Note: Fleishmann's unsalted margarine sticks are a great substitute for butter, for those on a dairy-free diet.

Refrigerator Coconut Cake

...a very special cake for special occasions.
This cake is made 3 days in advance and refrigerated
to allow the cake to become moist and the flavors to meld.

2½ cups sorghum flour mix
1 teaspoon xanthan gum
2 teaspoons baking soda
½ teaspoon salt
½ cup margarine or butter
2 cups packed brown sugar
3 eggs
1½ teaspoons pure vanilla extract
1 cup GF vanilla yogurt
1 cup lemon-lime carbonated beverage
Baking spray

Preheat oven to 350 degrees. Spray two 9-inch cake pans with GF baking spray.

Combine first 4 ingredients in small bowl.

Cream the margarine or butter in a large mixing bowl. Add the eggs alternately with sugar, one at a time, beating well after each addition. Add the vanilla. Add the dry ingredients alternately with the yogurt and carbonated beverage. Divide batter between the two prepared pans. Bake about 40 minutes or until a tester comes out clean. Cool on wire racks.

Split each cake into two layers using a long serrated knife.

Place the first layer on a cake plate and frost top only with filling. Add the second layer and frost top only, and then repeat with the third layer. Place the fourth layer on top and add 8-ounces non-dairy whipped topping to the reserved cup of filling. Use this to frost top of fourth layer as well as the sides of the cake. Place in well-sealed cake keeper. Refrigerate for 3 days.

For filling combine:
1 cup granulated sugar
2 cups sour cream
2 (12-ounce) packages frozen coconut, thawed

Makes one 9-inch round layered cake

Pumpkin Mini-Chip Cake

Make this cake in the Fall to treat family and friends.

2¾ cups sorghum flour mix
3 teaspoons baking powder
1½ teaspoons baking soda
1 teaspoon xanthan gum
½ teaspoon guar gum
2 teaspoons cinnamon
1 teaspoon ginger
1¾ teaspoons allspice
¼ teaspoon cloves
½ teaspoon nutmeg
1 teaspoon salt
1 cup granulated sugar
1 cup packed brown sugar
¾ cup canola oil
½ cup apple cider
4 large eggs
1 (15-ounce) can pure pumpkin puree
1 tablespoon pure vanilla extract
1¼ cups semi-sweet mini chocolate chips

Preheat oven to 350 degrees. Generously spray three 8-inch round pans with GF baking spray.

Whisk the first eleven ingredients together in a medium bowl; set aside.

In large mixing bowl beat the sugars, oil, and cider until creamy. Add the eggs one at a time, beating well after each addition. Add pumpkin and vanilla, mixing until combined. Add the flour mixture, mixing just until incorporated. Stir in mini-chips. Divide the batter between the three prepared pans. Bake 25 - 30 minutes or until a tester comes out clean. Cool 2 minutes then invert the cakes onto wire racks to finish cooling. Allow cake to completely cool; frost with Cream Cheese Frosting, page 111.

Store in an airtight cake-keeper. Refrigerate after the second day.

Yield: One 8-inch round layered cake

Pineapple Upside-Down Cake

Reminisce of grandmother's cooking with this cast iron favorite.
Light, not too sweet, and easy… prepare this cake in about 30 minutes!

¼ cup butter
¼ cup packed light brown sugar
7 canned pineapple rings, plus ½ cup reserved juice
7 frozen pitted cherries, thawed
2 cups sorghum flour mix
¾ cup sugar
1 teaspoon xanthan gum
1 tablespoon baking powder
1 teaspoon salt
1 egg
2 tablespoons canola oil
½ cup milk

Preheat oven to 350 degrees.

Melt the butter in a 10-inch cast iron skillet in the oven while the oven is preheating. Remove skillet from oven, tilt the pan to spread the butter evenly over the bottom of pan, then sprinkle the brown sugar evenly over the butter. Place the seven pineapple rings on top of the brown sugar and place a cherry in the center of each ring, halved side down.

Combine the flour mix, sugar, xanthan gum, baking powder, and salt in a small bowl. In a separate small bowl, whisk the egg, oil, milk, and reserved pineapple juice. Stir the egg mixture into the flour mixture until well combined. Spoon the batter by dollops onto the pineapples. Spread batter evenly with the back of a spoon. Bake 23 minutes or until tester comes out clean and top is lightly brown. Cool cake for 2-3 minutes before inverting onto a large round serving platter.

Serves 6-8

Frosting

Decorator Frosting

Use this frosting for decorating cakes. Add more powdered sugar for a firmer frosting (roses, borders, etc.) and less powdered sugar for frosting the actual cake. This frosting can be made dairy-free by substituting margarine or shortening for the butter. For a pure white frosting, use shortening instead of butter, and omit the pure vanilla extract.

1 teaspoon salt
1 tablespoon pure almond extract
1 tablespoon pure vanilla extract
½ cup water
½ cup butter, or shortening, or margarine
2 pounds powdered sugar

In a large mixing bowl combine the salt, flavorings, and water. Stir to dissolve salt. Add butter and 2 cups of powdered sugar; mix on low speed to combine. Add remaining powdered sugar, 2 cups at a time, beating after each addition until frosting is desired thickness. Beat on high until smooth and fluffy. Add food coloring, if desired, and mix until well incorporated.

Extra frosting can be stored in the refrigerator for up to 6 months.

Fluffy White Frosting

1 cup granulated sugar
¼ cup water
2 tablespoons light corn syrup
2 egg whites at room temperature
¼ cup sifted powdered sugar
1 teaspoon pure vanilla extract

Combine first 3 ingredients in a heavy saucepan; cook over medium heat, stirring constantly, until clear. Cook, without stirring, until candy thermometer reaches 236 degrees.

Beat egg whites until soft peaks form; continue to beat, slowly adding syrup mixture. Add powdered sugar and vanilla; continue beating until stiff peaks form and frosting is thick enough to spread.

Yield: 2½ cups

Chocolate Frosting

This old fashioned frosting will finish a birthday cake with rave reviews every time!

3-ounces good-quality semisweet chocolate, melted and cooled
¾ cups powdered sugar
1 tablespoon plus 1 teaspoon unsweetened cocoa
Pinch of salt
2-ounces cream cheese, softened
6 tablespoons unsalted butter, softened
¼ cup sour cream

Sift sugar, cocoa, and salt into a large bowl; set aside.

Beat cream cheese and butter in a mixing bowl until fluffy. Reduce speed to low. Add sugar mixture and mix well. Mix in melted chocolate and sour cream. Use immediately, or refrigerate airtight up to 2 days. Bring refrigerated frosting to room temperature and stir before using.

Frosts one 13 x 9-inch cake

Cream Cheese Frosting

1 (8-ounce) package cream cheese
1 stick unsalted butter or Fleishmann's unsalted margarine sticks
1 teaspoon salt
1 tablespoon pure vanilla extract
About 6 cups powdered sugar
1 teaspoon salt

Add cream cheese, butter or margarine, and salt to the bowl of an electric mixer and beat until smooth. Add vanilla. Add powdered sugar gradually, beating after each addition until fluffy and smooth.

Frosts one 13 x 9-inch cake

Quick Caramel Frosting

2 (14-ounce) cans sweetened condensed milk
½ cup packed light brown sugar
½ cup granulated sugar
1 teaspoon pure vanilla extract

Place all ingredients in a heavy 3-quart saucepan; bring to a boil, stirring constantly, 3 to 5 minutes or until mixture reaches a pudding-like thickness. Remove from heat.

Variations:
Quick Caramel-Pecan Frosting:
Prepare recipe above as directed; remove from heat and stir in 1½ cups shopped toasted pecans.

Quick Caramel-Coconut-Pecan Frosting:
Prepare frosting above as directed; remove from heat, stir in 1½ cups sweetened flaked coconut and 1½ cups chopped toasted pecans.

Pies
and
Pastry

Pastry Tips

For a pie requiring a baked filling (such as Apple Pie), prebake crust 10 minutes at 375 degrees, then fill with pie filling. Roll-out remaining dough between two sheets of sprayed plastic wrap. Remove top sheet of plastic wrap, cut dough into strips or shapes using a cookie cutter. Place strips or shapes on top of filling as desired. Adjust oven temperature according to pie instructions, then return pie to oven to complete the baking time.

For a pie that does not require a baked filling (such as custard) bake pastry 12-14 minutes at 375 degrees. Cool pastry before filling.

Rolling-out GF pastry
Roll-out pastry between two sheets of plastic wrap sprayed with GF baking pray. Remove top sheet of plastic wrap. Place upside-down pie pan on top of crust. With one hand on the bottom of the pie plate, and one hand under the bottom sheet of plastic wrap, flip the pan and pie crust over. Remove plastic wrap. Flute edges, adding extra crust if necessary.

Or

Pat-out crust directly into pie pan, making sure bottom of crust is thin and even.

Coconut Cream Pie

Here in the South, comfort, hospitality, and Coconut Cream Pie are synonymous. Try this one on for size, and go ahead, serve it to your guests...they will never suspect that it is gluten-free.

Dough for a single-crust pie pastry
¾ cup granulated sugar, divided
¼ cup cornstarch
2 cups half and half
4 egg yolks
3 tablespoons butter
1 cup dried flaked coconut, plus more for garnish
2½ teaspoons pure vanilla extract, divided
2 cups whipping cream

Choose a pastry recipe (see pages 120-124). Roll out pie crust, place in a 9-inch pie plate and bake according to instructions.

Combine ½ cup sugar and cornstarch in a heavy saucepan. In a separate bowl, whisk together half-and-half and egg yolks. Gradually whisk egg mixture into sugar mixture. Bring to a boil over medium heat, whisking constantly. Boil 1 minute, then remove from heat. Stir in butter, 1 cup coconut, and 1 teaspoon vanilla extract. Cover with plastic wrap, placing plastic wrap directly on filling in pan; let stand 30 minutes.

Spoon the custard mixture into the cooled crust; cover and chill 30 minutes or until set.

Beat whipping cream at high speed with an electric mixer until foamy; gradually add ¼ cup sugar and remaining 1½ teaspoons vanilla, beating until soft peaks form. Spread or pipe whipped cream over pie filling. Garnish with toasted coconut if desired.

Serves 6 to 8

Sweetheart Cherry Pie

Use the pie crust recipe below or Memaw's Pastry on page 181 for this delicious pie…see the photo on insert page H.

1 cup granulated sugar
4 tablespoons cornstarch
¼ teaspoon salt
¼ teaspoon cinnamon
½ teaspoon vanilla powder
2 pounds frozen pitted cherries, partially thawed

Pie Crust Ingredients:
1¾ cups fine white rice flour
1 cup sorghum flour mix
2 teaspoons granulated sugar
1¼ teaspoons salt
2¼ sticks (18 tablespoons) unsalted butter, cut into small pieces
4 - 6 tablespoons ice water

Preheat oven to 350 degrees. Spray a 9 or 10-inch pie plate with GF baking spray.

Prepare pie crust by pulsing flours, sugar, and salt in a food processor fitted with the knife blade. Add butter, and process until mixture resembles coarse meal, about 10 seconds. With machine running, add ice water in a slow, steady stream through the feed tube just until dough holds together (no longer than 30 seconds). Divide dough into thirds. Pat two thirds of the dough into and up the sides of the pie plate, evenly. Add extra dough to the top edge and flute. Bake 10 minutes. Remove pastry from the oven and then increase oven temperature to 375 degrees.

Meanwhile, combine sugar, cornstarch, salt, cinnamon, and vanilla powder in a large bowl; stir to combine. Add partially frozen cherries and stir well until cherries are evenly coated. Pour cherries into the partially baked pie shell.

Roll out remaining one third of dough between two pieces of plastic wrap, sprayed with GF baking spray. Remove top piece of plastic wrap and cut out shapes, such as hearts, with cookie cutters. Place hearts on top of cherries, leaving small areas uncovered. Place pie on a foil-lined baking sheet. Bake 1 hour. Cool on a wire rack. Pie can be stored at room temperature, tented with foil, for up to 1 day.

Apple Pie
with Crumb Topping

7 medium Granny Smith apples, peeled, cored, and sliced very thin
½ cup granulated sugar
1 teaspoon cinnamon
¼ teaspoon nutmeg
¼ teaspoon salt

Combine all above ingredients in a large mixing bowl; stir well and set aside.

Preheat oven to 400 degrees.

Prepare Sweet Pie Crust, page 122.

Stir apple mixture again and pour into an unbaked pie shell. Sprinkle crumb topping over apples. Lightly cover pie with foil to prevent topping from burning. Place pie plate on a foil-lined baking sheet in case juices run over.

Bake for 45 minutes or until center of pie is bubbling.

Crumb Topping:
¾ cup packed brown sugar
¾ cup sorghum flour mix
½ teaspoon nutmeg
6 tablespoons butter, cut into small pieces

In a small bowl combine brown sugar, flour mix, and nutmeg. Cut in butter with fork or pastry blender.

Easy as Apple Pie

This pie is a good "first" recipe for kids learning to cook. Kids can do a lot in the kitchen but adults should handle dangerous things like boiling water, the oven, and sharp knives.

7 Granny Smith or Fuji apples
½ cup raisins, optional
¾ cup plus 1 tablespoon granulated sugar
½ cup butter or margarine, softened
1½ cups sorghum flour mix
1 tablespoon heavy cream
1 teaspoon cinnamon

Preheat oven to 375 degrees. Spray a 13 x 9-inch baking dish with gluten-free baking spray.

An adult should peel, core, and slice apples into ¼-inch slices. Kids can cover the bottom of the prepared baking dish evenly with apple slices and sprinkle raisins over the apples.

In a large mixing bowl, beat ¾ cup sugar and the butter on medium speed for 4 - 5 minutes or until light and fluffy. Add the egg and then the 1½ cups flour, mixing well.

Sprinkle the dough as evenly as possible over the apples. Brush top of dough with cream.

In a small bowl, stir together the remaining tablespoon of sugar and cinnamon. Sprinkle mixture over crust. An adult should place the pan in the oven. Bake 15 minutes, then reduce the temperature to 350 degrees and bake the pie for 30 - 35 minutes longer, or until the crust is golden brown and the apples are bubbly. Serve warm.

Serves 6

Easy Frozen Lemonade Pie

Cool-off with a lemonade pie! Substitute pink lemonade for a pink pie!

1 (6-ounce) can frozen lemonade, thawed
1 (14-ounce) can sweetened condensed milk
1 (13½-ounce) tub frozen non-dairy whipped topping
1 GF graham cracker crust

Place first three ingredients in a large mixing bowl; mix until combined. Pour into baked and cooled graham cracker crust. Freeze at least 4 hours.

Freezer Strawberry Pie

*Pictured on insert page H, this pie is an
easy-to-prepare, light, summer treat.*

1 baked GF graham cracker crust
1 (16-ounce) package frozen strawberries, partially thawed
½ cup granulated sugar
1 unbeaten egg white
2 teaspoons lemon juice
1 (8-ounce) tub non-dairy whipped topping

Combine strawberries, sugar, egg white, and lemon juice in a large mixing bowl. Beat until soft peaks form, 5 - 8 minutes using the paddle attachment. Fold in the non-dairy whipped topping. Fill pie shell. Freeze until ready to serve.

Serves 8

Rich Delicious Chocolate Pie

Combine all ingredients in one bowl and beat until the mixture is light and fluffy…no baking required! Serve with whipped cream and a sprinkling of cocoa if desired.

1 cup butter, softened
1½ cups granulated sugar
4 (1-ounce) squares unsweetened chocolate, melted and cooled
1 teaspoon pure vanilla extract
4 egg whites
1 (9-inch) pie crust, baked and cooled

In a mixing bowl, beat butter and sugar until light and fluffy. Blend in chocolate and vanilla.

Add eggs, one at a time, beating 5 minutes after each egg is added. (This step is very important). Spoon mixture into the baked and cooled pie shell and chill.

Yield: One 9-inch pie

Butter Pastry

This traditional pastry will suit a variety of pies and please the most discriminating palates.

1¾ cup fine white rice flour
1 cup sorghum flour mix
2 teaspoons granulated sugar
1¼ teaspoon salt
2¼ sticks (18 tablespoons) unsalted butter, cut into small pieces
4-6 tablespoons water

Preheat oven to 350 degrees.

Spray a 10-inch pie plate with baking spray.

Pulse flours, sugar, and salt in a food processor to combine. Add butter and process until mixture resembles coarse meal, about 10 seconds. Add ice water through the chute in a slow steady stream, while pulsing, just until dough holds together (no longer than 20 seconds).

Divide dough in half. Set aside one half of dough.

Roll-out or pat other half into prepared pie plate (see pastry tips, page 113).

Yield: One double-layer pie crust

Memaw's Pastry

A traditional pie crust that is non-dairy.

2 cups sorghum flour mix
½ cup sweet white rice flour
1½ teaspoons salt
1 cup shortening
¼ cup ice water

Preheat oven to 400 degrees.

Spray a 10-inch pie plate with GF baking spray.

Combine flour and salt in a medium bowl. Cut-in shortening, adding water gradually. Add three more tablespoons of water, gradually, if necessary. Divide dough in half. Set one half of dough aside.

Roll-out or pat-out other half of pastry (see pastry tips on page 113). Place in prepared pie plate. Bake 10 minutes. Fill pie with filling. Roll-out remaining dough between two sheets of sprayed plastic wrap. Remove top sheet of plastic, cut dough into strips, or cut pastry into shapes using a cookie cutter. Place strips or shapes on filling. Bake according to pie instructions.

Or, if your pie does not require baking (such as Frozen Strawberry Pie) bake pie crust 15 minutes. Cool crust before filling.

Yield: One double-crust pastry

Sweet Pie Crust

1½ cups sorghum flour mix
¼ cup plus 1 tablespoon cornstarch
¼ cup sugar
1 teaspoon xanthan gum
8 tablespoons butter, cut up
1 large egg
1 teaspoon pure vanilla extract

Preheat oven to 400 degrees.

Lightly spray a 9-inch glass pie plate with GF baking spray.

In a large mixing bowl, stir together the flour and cornstarch. Add the sugar, butter, egg, and vanilla. Mix with fork or pastry blender until combined. (Do not over mix. Pastry should have a "marbled" effect.)

Divide into two balls. If only making a single crust pie, wrap one ball in plastic wrap and place in the freezer for later use.

Place the other ball between two pieces of plastic wrap, sprayed with GF baking spray. (Both pieces of plastic wrap should have sprayed-side turned toward the dough).

Roll the dough with a rolling pin, or a non-rimmed glass turned on its side, until it is ¼-inch thick. Remove top layer of plastic wrap. Lift bottom layer of plastic wrap and invert crust onto pie plate. Bake pastry for 7-8 minutes, fill with desired fruit filling, then bake according to pie directions. Or, for a no-bake pie, bake pie crust for 10 minutes, cool pastry completely, and then fill.

Makes one 9-inch single or double crust pastry

Pretzel Pie Crust

Start with GF store-bought pretzels and crushed pecans for an easy, light, delicious crust for fruit pies, custard pies, or pudding pies.

3 egg whites
¼ teaspoon cream of tartar
½ cup granulated sugar
1 teaspoon pure vanilla extract
1 cup crushed pecans
1 cup crushed GF pretzels

Preheat oven to 350 degrees.

Beat egg whites and cream of tartar in a mixing bowl until stiff. Add remaining ingredients and stir to combine. Spread evenly in a 10-inch pie plate sprayed with GF baking spray. Bake 28-30 minutes; cool before filling.

Yield: One 10-inch pie crust

Coconut Crust

Use this crust for a chocolate cheesecake, pudding fillings, or a fruit filling topped with whipped cream!

1 cup flaked coconut
½ cup store-bought GF gingersnap cookie crumbs
½ cup GF graham cracker crumbs (see note below)
¼ cup margarine, melted

Preheat oven to 350 degrees.

Combine all ingredients, mixing well. Firmly press into the bottom of a 9-inch springform pan or an 8-inch pie pan. Bake 5-7 minutes. Cool before filling with fruit or custard.

Yield: one 8 or 9-inch pie

Note: Make your own great graham crackers with the recipe Animal Grahams, page 88

Pie Crust Chart

Simply crush the store-bought gluten-free cookie varieties listed below, combine them with the other ingredients and pat into an 8 or 9-inch pie pan. Bake the pie crust according to the chart and then allow it to cool completely before filling with fruit or custard.

Finely Crushed Cookies -	Melted Butter	Sugar	Salt	Bake at 350 degrees
Gingersnap 1¼ cups	3 Tbsps	1Tbsp	¼ tsp	10 min
Chocolate 1½ cups	4 Tbsps	3 tsps	¼ tsp	8-10 min
Lemon 1½ cups	4 Tbsps	None	¼ tsp	8-10 min
Coconut 1½ cups	2 Tbsps	4 tsps	¼ tsp	9-10 min
Shortbread 1½ cups	4 Tbsps	3 tsps	¼ tsp	8-10 min
Graham Cracker 1½ cups	¼ cup	None		10 min

For testing purposes, I used Mi-Del GF Gingersnaps and Pamela's Chocolate, Lemon, and Shortbread cookies. I used homemade *Slice-n-Bake Coconut Tea Cookies,* page 87, for the coconut crumbs and *Animal Grahams,* page 88, for the graham cracker crumbs. Homemade graham crackers are great to have on hand for pie crusts. The recipe *Animal Grahams,* page 88, makes two 11 x 17-inch pans of crisp, delicious graham crackers. Snack on one pan of grahams and freeze the other for quick and easy pie-making. Graham crackers store best in an airtight tin, both at room temperature and in the freezer. Also, try homemade graham cracker crumbs in the *Coconut Crust* variation, page 123.

Snacks

Savory Crackers

These crackers are made with grapeseed oil which is low in saturated fat, contains no cholesterol, no trans-fatty acids, and is non-hydrogenated. It contains valuable antioxidants and is high in Vitamin E. Studies have shown it may raise good cholesterol and lower bad cholesterol, the effect of which may lower your risk of cardiovascular disease. Grapeseed oil has a high smoke point which means you can sauté, fry, or bake with it without it smoking or burning. And its excellent emulsification properties make it ideal for creamy dressings that will not separate when chilled. These crackers also allow healthy snacking without yeast.
Try them with soups, taco salads, or bean salads.

1 cup fine white rice flour
2 cups Masa Harina
½ cup raw sunflower seeds or sesame seeds
1 tablespoon non-fat dry buttermilk powder
2 tablespoons non-fat dry milk powder
2 teaspoons salt
¼ teaspoon paprika
¾ teaspoon cayenne powder
1 teaspoon garlic powder
¼ teaspoon cumin powder
½ cup grapeseed oil
1½ cups water

Preheat oven to 400 degrees.

Generously spray two jellyroll pans (11 x 17-inch) with GF baking spray.

Combine dry ingredients in large mixing bowl. Mix to combine. Add wet ingredients and beat until well blended. Batter will be thin.

Divide dough between the two prepared pans. Spread evenly to the edges of pan with a rubber spatula. Score with knife. Bake 20 minutes or until crispy and slightly brown. Remove from pan. Cool completely before storing in an airtight container.

Makes two 11 x 17-inch pans of crackers

Quesadillas

Quesadillas make a great quick snack or lunch and the varieties are endless! Tortillas for this recipe can be purchased or made from scratch. More varieties in GF corn tortillas are now available, such as those made from white corn, yellow corn, and blue corn, as well as GF tortillas made from brown rice flour and teff flour.

GF flour or corn tortillas
Olive, canola, or grapeseed oil
GF turkey, chicken, ham, or beef sliced thin from the deli
Grated Colby-jack cheese

Heat an electric skillet or cast iron skillet to medium-hot. Oil one side of each tortilla, stacking them "oiled sides together." Place meat and cheese slices on each top tortilla. Pick up top tortilla and place it on the hot skillet; top with remaining tortilla, oiled side out. Cook for about 40 seconds or until nicely brown and crisp. Turn tortilla and cook on second side about 40 seconds more. Remove from heat, slice into quarters and serve with desired dips.

Great dips for quesadillas include sour cream, guacamole, and salsa. Try Chunky Guacamole on page 278, and Salsa Fresca on page 268.

Also, try these variations:
- Honey mustard sauce served with a ham and Swiss or a ham and Muenster quesadilla
- Bar-B-Q sauce on a beef and Cheddar quesadilla
- Pasta sauce on a pepperoni and Mozzarella quesadilla

Candied Pumpkin Seeds

Pepitas (small green pumpkin seeds) are one of the most nutritious seeds around. They are very high in manganese, magnesium, and phosphorus but are also a good source of iron, tryptophan, vitamin K, iron, zinc, and protein. Nuts and seeds are a naturally rich source of phytosterols, believed to reduce blood levels of cholesterol and enhance immune response. They also contain cardio-protective fiber and the healthy kinds of fat. Eat them by the handful or sprinkle on top of a mixed green salad…see Citrus Salad with Candied Pumpkin Seeds, page 254. Also try Pumpkin Seed Tomatillo Sauce, page 267! Big Batch Granola and Granola Bars, from The Complete Book of Gluten-Free Cooking, are two great recipes to help you incorporate pumpkin seeds into the diet, as well.

2 cups raw pepitas
½ cup packed brown sugar
¼ cup granulated sugar
½ teaspoon salt
3 tablespoons orange juice

Preheat oven to 325 degrees. Spray a jellyroll (11 x 17-inch) pan with GF baking spray.

Combine all ingredients in a zip-top bag. Seal bag and mix well by turning and kneading the bag. Empty the pepitas onto the prepared pan. Bake for 12 minutes. Store in an airtight container for up to 3 months.

Apple-Cranberry Fruit Leather

My children love the store-bought fruit leather that has no food coloring, preservatives, or added sugar. I was pleased to discover I could make it at home for a fraction of the cost. This is our favorite version but you can try substituting blueberries for the cranberries, or pears in place of the apples. Bruised or over-ripe fruit works fine.

3 pounds baking apples (about 5 or 6 medium) such as Cameo, Braeburn, Fuji, or Gala, peeled, cored, and chopped (about 8 cups)
1 cup frozen cranberries, thawed
¼ cup pasteurized apple juice or cider
1 tablespoon plus 1 teaspoon fresh lemon juice
3 tablespoons honey
3 tablespoons granulated sugar

Preheat oven to 200 degrees.

Generously spray an 11 x 17-inch jellyroll pan.

Working in batches, puree apples, cranberries, apple juice or cider, lemon juice, honey, and sugar in a blender or food processor. Pour into a bowl to combine.

Pour puree in prepared pan; smooth with offset spatula. Bake about 4 -6 hours until dry to the touch (but not browned).

Remove fruit leather from pan and cut into desired size. Wrap in plastic wrap, place in airtight container, and store in refrigerator for up to 1 month.

Puppy Chow

*Here's an old favorite that can be enjoyed once again,
thanks to General Mills Rice Chex cereal,
which at the time of this printing is gluten-free.*

½ cup butter or margarine
1 cup peanut butter
1 (12-ounce) bag semi-sweet chocolate chips
1 (12-ounce) box GF rice squares cereal

Microwave butter or margarine, peanut butter, and chocolate chips for about 1 minute, or until completely melted, stirring frequently. Pour over 12-ounces of cereal. Stir gently, coating cereal completely. Pour 1 cup powdered sugar in gallon zip-top bag. Add some of the cereal, close bag and shake until the cereal is completely coated. Continue until all cereal is coated, adding more powdered sugar as needed. Allow puppy chow to completely cool on the baking sheet. Store in an airtight container.

Popcorn Balls

4 quarts popped popcorn
3 tablespoons unsalted butter
1 teaspoon salt
1 (10-ounce) bag GF marshmallows
6 ounces GF white chocolate
½ cup sliced almonds

Melt butter in a large pan over low heat. Add salt, marshmallows, and chocolate; cook, stirring until melted. Remove from heat; stir in almonds and popcorn. Shape into balls using a 2-inch ice-cream scoop coated with baking spray. Transfer to baking sheets lined with parchment paper. Let stand 30 minutes.

Yield: 56 popcorn balls

Pizza

Cast Iron Skillet Pizza

This particular recipe combines the nutrition of sorghum and corn and yields a crisp crust.

1½ teaspoons dry yeast
½ teaspoon granulated sugar
1¼ cups warm water
¼ cup unsalted butter, softened
3 cups GF sorghum flour mix
1 cup corn meal
2 teaspoons salt
4 cloves garlic, thinly sliced
½ cup Kalamata olives, pits removed, chopped
1 cup quartered artichoke hearts
4 Roma tomatoes, thinly sliced
12 ounces whole milk Mozzarella cheese, shredded
¼ cup pine nuts
2 tablespoons extra virgin olive oil, plus more for oiling the bowl and
    skillet, divided
½ cup basil leaves, torn into pieces

Preheat the oven to 500 degrees.

In the bowl of an electric mixer, combine the yeast, sugar, and water and let stand 5 minutes until foamy. Add the butter, flour, corn flour, and salt. Combine well, using the paddle attachment. Add 1 - 2 tablespoons water if the dough is dry and not coming together; add 1 - 2 tablespoons flour mix if the dough is too wet.

Oil two 9 or 10-inch cast iron skillets with olive oil. Divide dough between skillets and pat into the bottom of skillet and up the sides about one inch. Scatter dough with garlic, olives, artichokes, and tomatoes. Top with cheese and pine nuts. Drizzle each pizza with a tablespoon of olive oil. Bake on bottom rack of oven for 15 minutes. Reduce temperature to 400 degrees and bake until pizza crust is golden brown and toppings are starting to brown, 10 to 15 minutes. Remove pizza from the oven and top with basil.

Note: Toppings like pepperoni should be added when the oven temperature is reduced to 400 degrees to prevent burning.

Yield: Makes two 9 or 10-inch pizzas

Thin Pizza Crust

1½ cups tapioca flour
1 cup white rice flour
½ cup plus 1 tablespoon navy bean flour
½ cup plus 1 tablespoon sorghum flour
1 teaspoon xanthan gum
1 teaspoon salt
1 cup milk
3½ teaspoons dry yeast
4 teaspoons granulated sugar
3 large or 4 medium egg whites
6 tablespoons olive oil, divided

In a large mixing bowl, whisk together the tapioca flour, white rice flour, bean flour, sorghum flour, xanthan gum, and salt.

In a small saucepan over moderate heat, stir together milk and ½ cup milk; heat until warm but not hot to the touch, about 1 minute. Stir in yeast and sugar. Add milk-yeast mixture, egg whites, and 2 tablespoons olive oil to the dry ingredients and beat at medium speed with paddle attachment, scraping bowl occasionally, until dough is very smooth and very thick, about 5 minutes.

Spray four, 10-inch pizza pans with GF baking spray.

Preheat oven to 400 degrees.

Divide dough between pans, drizzle with olive oil and pat with oiled fingertips until dough forms a 10-inch diameter pizza crust, ¼ inch thick. Bake each crust for 5 to 10 minutes depending on desired crispness. Baked crusts can be made ahead, wrapped in plastic wrap and frozen, up to 1 month. Thaw in 350 degree oven until hot, 4 - 5 minutes, before topping and broiling.

To top and broil pizzas:
Preheat broiler. Top pizzas with desired toppings and broil, about 4 inches from heat, rotating as needed for even browning, until cheese is bubbling and crust is golden brown, 4 - 6 minutes. Slice and serve immediately.

Yield: Four 10-inch pizzas

Pizza or Calzone Dough

Our family's favorite pizza dough, this recipe makes two thin-crust 12-inch pizzas or three 8-inch calzones.

1 tablespoon dry yeast
1½ cups warm milk
1 teaspoon granulated sugar
2½ cups sorghum flour mix
3 teaspoons guar gum
1 teaspoon salt
1 teaspoon dried oregano
2 teaspoons olive oil
2 teaspoons apple cider vinegar

Preheat oven to 425 degrees. Spray two 12-inch pizza pans with GF baking spray.

In a small bowl, dissolve yeast and sugar in warm milk.

In a large mixing bowl, blend together flour, guar gum, salt, and oregano. Add yeast mixture to dry ingredients, mixing well. Add olive oil and apple cider vinegar. Beat on high 2 minutes.

Divide dough between the two pizza pans. Dip fingertips in olive oil and pat dough evenly. Allow dough to rise in a warm place for 45 minutes.

Preheat oven to 425 degrees. Bake pizzas for 11 minutes. Remove pizzas from oven and add toppings, then bake another 11 minutes.

For calzones, divide the dough into three 8-inch rounds, bake for 10 minutes, then place toppings on one half of each crust, fold the crust over, and bake another 10-12 minutes.

Yield: Two 12-inch pizzas or three 8-inch calzones

Egg-Free Pizza Crust

1 tablespoon quick rise yeast
2/3 cup brown rice flour
1/2 cup tapioca flour
1 tablespoon dry milk powder
1/2 teaspoon xanthan gum
1/2 teaspoon salt
1 teaspoon unflavored gelatin powder
2/3 cup warm water
1/2 teaspoon granulated sugar or 1/4 teaspoon honey
1 teaspoon olive oil
1 teaspoon cider vinegar

Preheat oven to 425 degrees.

Spray a 12-inch pizza pan with GF baking spray.

In mixing bowl, blend the yeast, flours, dry milk powder, xanthan gum, salt, and gelatin powder on low speed. Add warm water, sugar, olive oil, and vinegar. Beat on high speed for 3 minutes. Add a tablespoon of water if necessary. Pat dough into prepared pan with fingers oiled with olive oil, making edges slightly thicker and higher. Bake 17 - 20 minutes.

Remove from oven, add toppings and return to oven to bake another 10-12 minutes.

Yield: One 12-inch pizza

Variations:

- substitute 2/3 cup sorghum flour for brown rice flour

- substitute 1/3 cup sorghum flour plus 1/3 cup quinoa flour for brown rice flour

- substitute 1/3 cup sorghum flour plus 1/3 cup amaranth flour for brown rice flour

Calzones

3 cups calzone flour mix
2 teaspoons dry yeast
1 teaspoon xanthan gum
½ teaspoon salt
1 teaspoon garlic powder
1¾ cups warm water
2 eggs
1 tablespoon honey
2 tablespoons olive oil, plus more to oil pan

In large mixing bowl, combine dry ingredients. Add wet ingredients and beat on high using paddle attachment for 3 minutes. Cover with a dish towel and let rise for 2 hours in a warm place.

Heat a 10 - 12 inch cast iron skillet. Add 1 tablespoon olive oil to the skillet and swirl pan to spread evenly. Drop a large dollop of dough onto the skillet and spread-out with the back of a spatula until it is almost as big as the pan. Let cook 1-1½ minutes. Turn; cook another 1-2 minutes. Top one half with fillings such as cheese, pepperoni, ham/broccoli/cheese, grilled veggies, leftover steak & cheese, etc. Fold bread over filling; allow cheese to melt then remove to serving platter.

Yield: About 2 large calzones

Calzone Flour Mix
3 cups sorghum flour
½ cup yellow cornmeal
2½ cups cornstarch
1½ cups tapioca starch
Combine all ingredients in a zip-top bag. Label and refrigerate.
Makes 7½ cups mix.

Quick Mini Pizzas

Day-old hamburger buns or previously frozen buns work great for this quick snack or lunch.

Use the recipe for Super Sandwich Bread on page 42 to make hamburger buns. Place hamburger buns "open face" on a foil-lined baking sheet. Adjust oven rack to middle position. Broil buns until they begin to brown, about 2 minutes.

Remove from oven and top each half with pasta sauce, grated cheese, pepperoni, or other toppings, as desired. Return pizzas to the oven and broil until cheese melts, about 2-3 minutes longer. Watch pizzas closely and be sure not to leave the oven unattended while broiling.

Breakfast Pizza

...a scrumptious breakfast!

Pizza crust of choice (see recipes in this section)
6 eggs, beaten
½ pound bacon, cooked and crumbled
1 cup (4-ounces) shredded Cheddar cheese
1 (4-ounce) can sliced mushrooms, drained

Spray a 12-inch pizza pan with GF baking spray.

Prepare pizza crust according to directions, pat into pan, and prebake 10 minutes.

Meanwhile, whisk eggs, bacon, cheese, and mushrooms in a medium bowl; pour over prepared crust. Bake at 375 degrees for 12-15 minutes.

Yield: One 12-inch pizza

Chicken

Southwestern Chicken-Corn Cakes

...a fabulous recipe that is worth the extra time and effort.
See photo on back cover.

1 (11-ounce) can Mexican-style corn, drained
1 cup fine GF breadcrumbs, divided (I prefer Gillian's Foods breadcrumbs)
1 large egg
4 cups chopped chicken (leftover grilled chicken works well)
½ red and ½ green bell pepper, chopped
½ cup green onion
¼ cup GF mayonnaise
2½ teaspoons GF Dijon mustard
½ teaspoon pepper
1 teaspoon salt
2 teaspoons chopped fresh basil
2 teaspoons chopped fresh cilantro
Olive oil
Tomato, Basil, and Corn Relish
Yogurt Sauce

Preheat oven to 350 degrees. Lightly spray a 13 x 9-inch glass baking dish with GF baking spray.

Place ½ cup corn in a large bowl, reserving remaining corn in can for the relish. Add ½ cup breadcrumbs, 1 egg, chicken, and next 8 ingredients to corn in bowl; combine well. Shape mixture into 8 patties.

Dredge patties in remaining breadcrumbs, shaking to remove excess. In a large skillet over medium heat, fry patties in 2 - 3 tablespoons olive oil, about 1 minute each side, until browned. Remove from skillet and place in the prepared baking dish. Bake 15 minutes.

Meanwhile, prepare *Tomato Basil and Corn Relish* as well as the *Yogurt Sauce.*

Tomato, Basil, and Corn Relish
Reserved Mexican-style corn in can, drained
1½ cups seeded and chopped plum tomatoes
½ cup chopped red onion (I sauté my red onions until clear)
¼ cup chopped red or green bell pepper
2 tablespoons chopped fresh basil
1 tablespoon chopped fresh cilantro
1½ tablespoons red wine vinegar
1 tablespoon olive oil
Salt and pepper to taste

Combine all relish ingredients in a medium bowl, stirring well. Seal tightly and refrigerate until needed. Bring to room temperature before serving. Relish may be made up to two days in advance.

Yogurt Sauce
1 (6-ounce) container GF plain yogurt
½ cup GF mayonnaise
1 tablespoon GF Dijon mustard
1 teaspoon Worcestershire sauce
¼ teaspoon pepper
½ teaspoon sugar

Whisk together all yogurt sauce ingredients in a small lidded container. Seal tightly and refrigerate until needed. Sauce may be made up to 2 days in advance.

To assemble:
Arrange chicken patty on a lettuce leaf, top with Tomato, Basil, and Corn Relish, then drizzle with Yogurt Sauce.

Yield: 8 patties

Easy Tostado Casserole

You can find crisp tostado shells alongside other Mexican ingredients at many supermarkets.   Sturdy corn tortillas chips make an acceptable substitute. Leftover chicken, store-bought tostado shells, and a short bake time, make this a quick and easy dinner!

1 (28-ounce) can diced tomatoes, drained
1 small onion, chopped
3 garlic cloves, peeled
2 jalapeno peppers, seeded and chopped
2 tablespoons canola oil
2 cups shredded GF rotisserie chicken
¾ cup GF chicken broth
½ cup chopped fresh cilantro
Salt and pepper
15 corn tostados broken into pieces or 8 cups corn tortilla chips
2½ cups Monterey Jack cheese, shredded

Adjust oven rack to middle position and heat oven to 425 degrees. Spray a 2-quart casserole dish with gluten-free baking spray.   Puree tomatoes, onion, garlic, and peppers in a blender until smooth, about 1 minute.

Heat oil in a medium saucepan over medium heat.   Add tomato sauce, bring to a simmer, and cook until slightly thickened, 5 - 7 minutes.   Add chicken, broth, and cilantro and season with salt and pepper.

Place half of chips in prepared dish, top with half of sauce, half of chicken mixture, and half of cheese.   Repeat with a second layer.   Expose several chips on top layer so they can crisp in the oven.   Bake until bubbly and cheese begins to brown, 12 - 15 minutes.   Serve warm with sour cream.

Serves 6

Chili-Lime Chicken

½ cup olive oil
4 tablespoons fresh lime juice
2 tablespoons minced garlic
3 tablespoons cumin
2 tablespoons chili powder
6 large bone-in chicken breasts
Chopped cilantro

Create a marinade by whisking the first five ingredients in a bowl. (Reserve some of the marinade; store in the refrigerator.) Rub the chicken with the unreserved marinade and allow the chicken to marinate for 2 - 3 hours.

Heat a cast iron skillet on the stove. Sear the chicken in the hot skillet, 6 minutes on each side. Test with an instant-read thermometer; chicken should register 170 - 180 degrees.

Remove chicken from the skillet. Add remaining marinade to the skillet. Heat until garlic is fragrant. Scrape sauce into a bowl and add chopped cilantro; serve as a dipping sauce.

Buttermilk Baked Chicken

This recipe is great when you need to serve a crowd.

1 family pack chicken legs
1 family pack chicken thighs
2 cups buttermilk
4 tablespoons honey
Salt and pepper
1 (10.6-ounce) box GF cornflakes, crushed into crumbs

Remove skin from chicken. Place thighs in one gallon freezer zip-top bag and legs in a second zip-top bag. To each bag add 1 cup buttermilk, 2 tablespoons honey, salt and pepper. Zip bag, mix well, and place each bag in a bowl. Refrigerate at least 2 hours.

Preheat oven to 425 degrees. Discard marinade. Roll each piece of chicken in GF cornflake crumbs. Place on foil-lined baking sheet sprayed with baking spray. Bake about 1 hour.

Herb Roasted Chicken

Easy and delicious, this chicken works well with just about anything!
Fancy-it-up with a side of rice pilaf and steamed broccoli or,
satisfy the kids by pairing it with macaroni and cheese and
corn on the cob.

1 (4-5 pound) roasting chicken
1 teaspoon Herbs de Provence
½ teaspoon salt
½ teaspoon pepper
Dried orange peel

Preheat oven to 350 degrees.

Combine Herbs de Provence, salt, pepper, and orange peel in a small bowl.

Remove and discard giblets from chicken cavity; rinse with cold water, and pat dry. Loosen skin and rub seasonings under skin. Rub any remaining seasonings on top of skin. Place chicken, breast side up, in a Dutch oven.

Bake about 40-50 minutes or until a meat thermometer inserted into chicken thigh registers 175 degrees. Serve immediately.

Serves 4-5

*Vegetable
Pasta*

*Blueberry
Orange
Scones*

A

Wrap Bread

Chocolate Meringue Cookies

B

*Black Bean
& Spinach
Enchiladas*

Dutch Baby Pancake

C

Cream-Filled Chocolate Cupcakes

Nut Balls

D

Beef Jerky

&

*Granola
Bars*

Spritz Cookies

&

*Slice and Bake
Coconut Tea
Cookies*

E

Thai-Style Steak Salad

Apple Fritters

F

Delicate
Crispy
Almond
Cookies

Sour Cream
Coffee
Cake

Sweetheart Cherry Pie

Freezer Strawberry Pie and Éclairs

Roasted Pecan Chicken

Pecans, butter, fresh basil, and honey are spread under the skin of this chicken, slowly basting it as it roasts.

¼ cup unsalted butter
6 pecan halves
2 fresh basil leaves
2 tablespoons chopped green onions
1½ teaspoons honey
1 (4-pound) whole roasting chicken
1 lemon, halved
1 teaspoon salt
1 teaspoon pepper
4 slices Applewood smoked bacon
6 cloves garlic

Process first 5 ingredients in a food processor until smooth, stopping to scrape down sides. Set aside.

Remove and discard giblets from chicken cavity; rinse with cold water, and pat dry. Squeeze juice from 1 lemon half evenly over chicken; rub well with squeezed half. Repeat procedure with remaining lemon half of lemon inside chicken cavity. Reserve lemon halves.

Loosen and lift skin from chicken breasts with fingers; spread pecan mixture evenly underneath. Carefully replace skin. Sprinkle ½ teaspoon salt and ½ teaspoon pepper evenly on skin; rub into skin. Sprinkle remaining ½ teaspoon salt and ½ teaspoon pepper inside cavity; rub into cavity. Place bacon slices evenly over skin of chicken breasts. Insert garlic cloves and reserved lemon halves in cavity of chicken. Place chicken, breast side up, in a 10-inch cast-iron skillet.

Bake at 400 degrees for 20 minutes. Reduce oven temperature to 325 degrees, and bake 60 minutes or until a meat thermometer inserted into chicken thigh registers 175 degrees. Remove from oven, and let stand at room temperature until thermometer registers 180 degrees.

Serves 4-5

Crunchy Chicken Nuggets

1 pound boneless, skinless chicken breast, rinsed and patted dry
     with paper towels
1½ cups GF plain yogurt
3 cups crushed GF corn flakes
2 tablespoons fresh parsley, chopped
1 teaspoon salt
½ teaspoon pepper
Vegetable or olive oil for frying
Plastic or paper bag

Preheat oven to 375 degrees. Slice chicken breasts into 2-inch strips.
Marinate chicken pieces in yogurt for one hour or up to 24 hours,
refrigerated.

Spray an 11 x 17-inch jellyroll pan with GF baking spray.

Prepare the crunchy crust by combining the corn flakes, parsley, salt and
pepper in a bowl. Place corn flake mixture in a plastic or paper bag. Drop
chicken, a few pieces at a time, into the bag and shake thoroughly to coat.
Remove chicken pieces from bag, shaking excess mixture from each
piece. Place on the prepared pan. Bake about 25 minutes or until crunchy
on the outside and cooked through. Serve with warm honey mustard
sauce.

Honey Mustard Sauce
½ cup GF mayonnaise
2 tablespoons GF Dijon or spicy mustard
2 tablespoons honey

Combine all ingredients; stir well. To warm the sauce, place all ingredients
in a small saucepan, heat over medium heat, stirring often, just until warm.

Crispy Chicken Fingers

Only a small amount of oil is used to give these chicken fingers a brown, crusty exterior, then they are transferred to the oven to finish cooking.

1 cup sorghum flour mix
1 teaspoon salt
½ teaspoon pepper
1 cup lemon-lime carbonated beverage
2 pounds chicken tenders
GF plain breadcrumbs (I prefer Gillian Foods plain breadcrumbs)
Canola oil

Heat canola oil (½ - inch deep) in a tall, narrow stock pot or fryer. Preheat oven to 375 degrees.

Combine the first four ingredients in a medium bowl. Dredge chicken tenders in the mixture, then in breadcrumbs. Fry in hot oil for 30 seconds each side, remove with slotted spoon, then transfer to a baking dish and place it in the oven to keep warm until all chicken are finished frying. Leave chicken in the oven 15 minutes or until baked through. Serve with dipping sauce.

Fried Chicken Fingers

Though I don't fry food often, these chicken fingers are a great "once-in-a-while" treat and the best chicken fingers ever!

Boneless chicken tenders, or chicken breasts cut into cubes
Rice flour seasoned with salt and pepper
Eggs, beaten
GF breadcrumbs (I prefer Gillian's Foods plain breadcrumbs)
Canola oil

Heat oil (3 - inches deep) in a tall, narrow stock pot or fryer.

Place rice flour in a shallow bowl and season with salt and pepper.

In second shallow bowl, place beaten eggs.

Place breadcrumbs in third shallow bowl.

Dip chicken tenders in flour, followed by egg, then breadcrumbs. Fry in hot oil, in batches, until golden brown, about 2 minutes.

Chicken and Ham Rolls

3 whole chicken breasts (about 1½ pound) boned, skinned, and halved
6 thin slices baked ham
1 egg
1 tablespoon prepared GF mustard
¼ cup grated Parmesan cheese
½ teaspoon salt
¼ teaspoon white pepper
½ cup GF dried bread crumbs (I prefer Gillian's Foods plain breadcrumbs)
6 tablespoons butter or margarine

Sauce:
2 tablespoons butter or margarine
2 tablespoons cornstarch (may need a little more)
½ teaspoon salt
¼ teaspoon white pepper
1 tablespoon prepared GF mustard
1½ cups milk
½ cup dry white wine
1 cup grated Swiss cheese (4-ounce)

Preheat oven to 375 degrees. Line a 12 x 8 x 2-inch baking dish with foil and lightly spray with GF baking spray.

Wash chicken breasts; pat dry with paper towels. Pound chicken breasts, one at a time, ¼-inch thick between sheets of waxed paper. Place a slice of ham on each piece of chicken; roll up from the short end and secure with a toothpick.

Combine egg, 1 tablespoon mustard and 2 tablespoons water; mix well. In a separate bowl combine Parmesan cheese, ½ teaspoon salt, ¼ teaspoon pepper and the breadcrumbs. Dip chicken rolls in egg mixture, then in crumb mixture. Arrange in a singe layer in a 13 x 9-inch baking pan sprayed with GF baking spray. Spoon 1 tablespoon melted butter over each roll. Bake uncovered, 45 minutes, or until richly browned and fork tender.

Meanwhile, make the sauce. In small heavy saucepan, melt 2 tablespoons butter. Remove from heat. In a small bow, whisk cornstarch into milk. Add salt, pepper, and mustard. Add milk mixture to saucepan, gradually. Return to heat and bring to a boil, stirring constantly. Add wine and Swiss cheese; simmer, stirring 1 minute.

Pour ¾ of the sauce into the bottom of the foil-lined baking dish. Place chicken rolls on top. Pour remaining sauce over chicken rolls. If desired, sprinkle with extra shredded Swiss cheese. Place under broiler 1 minute.

Serves 6

Chicken with Sun-Dried Tomatoes and Fettuccini

Start with left-over cooked chicken or buy a GF rotisserie chicken for a quick, one-pot, delicious meal.

3 cloves garlic, minced
¼ cup olive oil
¼ cup margarine
1 teaspoon salt
½ - ¾ cups chopped sun-dried tomatoes
2 cups chopped cooked chicken
¼ cup white wine
2 tablespoons fresh chopped basil
1 (16-ounce) package GF fettuccine

Cook fettuccine in a large pot of salted water or chicken broth; drain pasta in a colander. In same pot, sauté garlic in margarine and olive oil until fragrant. Add remaining ingredients including fettuccini; toss well. Serve immediately.

Sundried Tomato-Basil Crusted Chicken

6 tablespoons butter or margarine
1 clove garlic, minced
4 sundried tomatoes, chopped
2 tablespoons chopped fresh basil
¾ cup plain GF breadcrumbs (I prefer Gillian Foods breadcrumbs)
¼ cup freshly grated Parmesan cheese
1 tablespoon sliced green onions or chives
4 (6-ounce) boneless chicken breasts

Preheat oven to 375 degrees. Spray a 13 x 9-inch baking dish with GF baking spray.

In a medium skillet melt 1 tablespoon of the butter over medium heat. Add garlic and cook 1 minute. Stir in tomatoes and basil and cook 1 minute longer. Add remaining butter and stir until melted. Remove from heat and stir in breadcrumbs, cheese, and onion or chives.

Pound chicken breasts thin; place in prepared pan. Divide breadcrumb mixture evenly over the chicken and press firmly. Bake 25 - 30 minutes or until chicken reaches 165 degrees on a meat thermometer.

Serves 4

Chicken or Turkey Divan

...a quick, easy recipe to use up leftover chicken or turkey!
Or, purchase a GF rotisserie chicken to debone.

3 cups cooked chicken or turkey chunks
2 (16-ounce) packages frozen broccoli spears, thawed
3 tablespoons butter
3 tablespoons sorghum flour mix
½ teaspoon salt
½ teaspoon pepper
1 cup plus 2 tablespoons milk (GF chicken broth for non-dairy version)
½ cup GF mayonnaise
Juice from 1 lemon
½ cup grated Parmesan cheese

Preheat oven to 350 degrees.

Melt butter over low heat. Blend in flour, salt, and pepper. Cook over low heat stirring until mixture is smooth and bubbly. Whisk in milk. Heat to boiling, stirring constantly. Whisk mayonnaise and lemon juice into the sauce. Remove from heat.

Arrange broccoli in sprayed casserole. Sprinkle chicken or turkey evenly over broccoli. Pour the sauce evenly over the chicken or turkey; sprinkle with Parmesan cheese. Bake 25 - 30 minutes.

Serves 6

Chicken and Celery Stir-Fry

1 pound boneless skinless chicken breast halves (about 2)
1 large egg white
1 tablespoon cornstarch
Salt and pepper
2 - 3 tablespoons canola oil
1 pound celery (8 - 10 stalks) thinly sliced on the diagonal
1 (3-inch) piece of fresh ginger, peeled and thinly sliced lengthwise
1 Poblano pepper, slivered lengthwise, seeds removed
3 tablespoons rice vinegar
1 teaspoon toasted sesame oil
1 tablespoon granulated sugar
4 green onions, chopped

Cut chicken into thin strips, 2½ - 3 inches long. In a quart size zip- top bag whisk together egg white, cornstarch, and 1 teaspoon each of salt and pepper until smooth. Add chicken strips, and toss to coat.

Heat 1 tablespoon oil in a large nonstick skillet over medium-high heat. Add half of coated chicken strips to the skillet; cook, turning once, until golden about 5 minutes. Transfer to a plate. Add another tablespoon vegetable oil to skillet and brown remaining chicken in same manner.

Add celery, ginger, and Poblano pepper to remaining oil in skillet (add more oil if necessary); cook, tossing, until celery is crisp-tender, 4 - 5 minutes.

Stir in vinegar, sesame oil, and sugar with the vegetables. Add green onions and cooked chicken; toss until combined and heated through, 1 - 2 minutes. Serve immediately.

Serves 4

Apricot-Glazed Chicken Breasts

1 (10 -12 ounce) jar apricot preserves
½ cup orange juice
3 tablespoons lemon juice
¼ cup quartered dried apricots
¾ teaspoon salt
¾ teaspoon pepper
4 split bone-in chicken breasts
2 teaspoons vegetable oil

Adjust oven rack to middle position and heat oven to 425 degrees. Whisk apricot preserves, orange juice, lemon juice, apricots, ¼ teaspoon salt, and ¼ teaspoon pepper together in a medium bowl. Season both sides of chicken breasts with remaining salt and pepper.

Heat oil in large skillet over medium-high heat until just smoking. Place chicken breasts, skin side down in skillet, and cook until well browned and most fat has rendered, 8 - 10 minutes. Turn chicken and lightly brown on second side, 2 to 3 minutes longer.

Transfer chicken to medium baking dish and set aside. Discard fat in skillet and add apricot mixture. Simmer vigorously over high heat, stirring constantly, until thick and syrupy, 3 - 4 minutes. Pour glaze over chicken and turn chicken skin side down.

Bake, turning chicken skin side up halfway through cooking, until thickest part of breast registers 160 degrees on an instant-read thermometer, about 12 - 16 minutes. Transfer chicken to a platter and let it rest 5 minutes. Meanwhile, transfer remaining glaze in baking dish to a small bowl. Serve chicken, passing extra glaze separately.

Serves 4

Barbeque Chicken Wings or Legs

I prefer chicken legs over wings but either way, these are great! The sauce can be made ahead and frozen. Extra sauce can be frozen as well.

30 chicken wings or 20 chicken legs, skin removed

Sauce Ingredients:
2 cups ketchup
½ cup cider vinegar
Juice of 1 lemon
2 tablespoons Worcestershire sauce
1 teaspoon Tabasco sauce
2 tablespoons unsulfured molasses
2 tablespoons spicy brown GF mustard
1 teaspoon chili powder
¼ cup packed brown sugar
1 teaspoon garlic powder

Combine all sauce ingredients in a medium saucepan and bring to a boil over medium heat. Reduce temperature to low and simmer, covered, for 30 minutes.

Preheat oven to 350 degrees. Spray a 13 x 9-inch casserole with GF cooking spray. Place the chicken pieces in a large bowl and toss with 1½ cups sauce. Lie chicken in a single layer in prepared dish and bake, 45-50 minutes. Serve with extra sauce.

Yield: 3 cups sauce
         30 wings or 20 legs

Chicken with Chipotle Barbeque Sauce

Chipotle peppers are smoked and dried jalapeno peppers.
They are commonly sold in a chunky paste called "adobo."
Serve this dish with *Classic Creamy Coleslaw* from *The Complete Book of Gluten-Free Cooking,* corn on the cob, and watermelon
for a fabulous summertime feast!

2 tablespoons chipotle peppers in adobo sauce
GF cooking spray
1 small onion, chopped
3 cloves garlic, minced
1 cup ketchup
3 tablespoons white wine vinegar
3 tablespoons molasses
1 tablespoon Worcestershire sauce
6 medium skinless, boneless chicken breast halves (about 1½ pounds)

Remove any stems from the chipotle peppers in adobo sauce. Place peppers and sauce in a blender or food processor. Cover, and process until smooth; set aside.

Lightly coat a medium sauce pan with cooking spray. Cook onion and garlic over medium-high heat for 2 - 3 minutes or until tender. Stir in chipotle mixture, ketchup, vinegar, molasses, and Worcestershire sauce. Bring to boiling; reduce heat. Simmer for 10 minutes, uncovered, stirring often.

Place chicken on grill over medium heat. Grill for 12 - 15 minutes or until instant-read thermometer inserted in center registers 170 degrees and juices run clear, turning once and brushing with the sauce several times during the last half of grilling.

Bring the remaining sauce just to boiling; serve with chicken.

Serves 6

Jerk Chicken

This Jamaican marinade, or jerk sauce, is traditionally used with pork or chicken.

3 green onions, chopped
2 garlic cloves, minced
1 - 2 jalapeno peppers, seeded and chopped
2 tablespoons fresh lime juice
2 tablespoons olive oil
1 tablespoon light-brown sugar
1½ teaspoons ground allspice
1 teaspoon dried thyme
½ teaspoon ground cinnamon
8 pieces bone-in chicken with skin

Prepare marinade in a blender or food processor combining green onions, garlic, jalapeno peppers, lime juice, oil, sugar, allspice, thyme, cinnamon, 1 teaspoon salt, and 2 tablespoons water. Blend until smooth. Set aside ¼ cup for brushing.

Place chicken in a shallow dish, season with salt. Loosen skin and spoon marinade under skin. Pour remaining marinade over chicken, coating well. Cover and refrigerate, turning once or twice, at least 2 hours, or overnight.

Heat grill to medium-high; oil grates. Lift chicken from marinade, discarding marinade. Place on grill and close grill lid. Cook, turning occasionally, until chicken is blackened in spots, about 10 minutes. Move chicken to cooler part of the grill; brush with reserved marinade. Grill, covered, until chicken is cooked through, about 15 minutes more. Serve immediately.

Serves 4-5

Beef

Meatloaf

1½ pounds lean ground beef
¾ cup GF dried breadcrumbs
1 carrot, grated
½ onion, chopped
1 garlic clove, minced
¾ cup GF chicken broth
1 egg
¼ cup GF ketchup
1 tablespoon dried basil
1 tablespoon GF Dijon mustard (I use Annie's Dijon mustard)
½ teaspoon salt
½ teaspoon pepper

Preheat oven to 350 degrees.

Combine all ingredients and mix well. Form into a loaf and place on a wire rack coated with baking spray. Place wire rack in a foil-lined 13 x 9-inch baking pan.

Bake 30 minutes or until center is no longer pink.

Serves 5

Slow-Cooker Sloppy Joes

…our family's favorite Sloppy Joe recipe, converted to gluten-free,
and just as tasty as the original!
This recipe makes enough for fast food (an extra meal in the freezer).

3 pounds ground beef
Salt and pepper
1 large onion, diced
3 cloves garlic, minced
1¼ cups barbeque sauce (I prefer Cattleman's Classic barbeque sauce)
1 (28-ounce) can tomato puree
1 (6-ounce) can tomato paste
2 tablespoons packed brown sugar

Brown meat in a skillet over medium-high heat, seasoning with salt and pepper; drain. Add meat to a slow-cooker with remaining ingredients, stirring well. Cook at high setting for 10 - 15 minutes, then turn to low setting and cook for 6 hours.

Serve with gluten-free hamburger buns.

Allow meat to completely cool before freezing.

Serves a family of 5, twice!

Old Fashioned
Bread Dressing

This is my grandmother's recipe for Thanksgiving dressing which I have converted with as few changes as possible. Thanksgiving would not be the same for our family without it.

20 cups dry bread cubes from Super Sandwich Bread
1 pound lean ground meat
¾ cup (1½ stick) Fleishmann's unsalted margarine
1 small onion
1 teaspoon pepper
1½ tablespoons salt (may need less if chicken broth is salted)
2 cups GF chicken broth
3 eggs

Preheat oven to 400 degrees.

Brown meat and onion in a saucepan over medium-high heat; season with salt and pepper; drain fat. Remove from heat and add margarine, stirring until melted. Place meat, breadcrumbs, and eggs in a buttered roaster or a foil-lined deep baking pan. Mix well. Cover and bake 2 hours, stirring every 30 minutes. Bake longer if bread is still mushy. If dressing seems too dry, add more chicken broth, ½ cup at a time, stirring well to incorporate.

To make breadcrumbs:
Use homemade gluten-free sandwich bread, such as Super Sandwich Bread and slice into ½ to 1-inch cubes. Spread cubes evenly on a jellyroll pan and bake 225 degrees until breadcrumbs have a crisp exterior and slightly soft interior. Breadcrumbs can be made in advance, stored in canning jars or freezer zip-top bags, and frozen until needed.

Serves 12

Balsamic Roast

Whip up some mashed potatoes to make the most of this roast's delicious gravy. If desired, add vegetables such as carrots and celery about 50 minutes before the end of cooking time.

1 (4-pound) chuck, rump, or eye of round roast
Fresh ground black pepper
2 large onions, sliced
1 cup balsamic vinegar
¾ cup GF soy sauce
½ cup water
½ cup packed brown sugar
1 cup GF beef broth
½ dry white wine
4 garlic cloves, minced
3-4 bay leaves

Preheat oven to 300 degrees.

Season roast with pepper. Place onions in high-sided roast pan or Dutch oven. Place roast on top of onions. Combine remaining ingredients and pour over roast.

Cover and bake 4 hours or until meat is tender and pulls apart easily.

For gravy:
Remove 2 cups of gravy from roast pan; skim off fat.

In small saucepan add 2 tablespoons cornstarch to ¼ cup cool water; whisk to combine. Whisk in the 2 cups of gravy. Heat over medium high heat until thickened; serve with roast.

Serves 6

Chicken Fried Steak

2 pieces (about 8" long and ¾" thick) flank steak, tenderized
1 teaspoon salt
1 teaspoon pepper
1 cup sorghum flour (not mix)
1 cup potato starch flour
¼ teaspoon baking soda in 1 cup water
Canola oil or olive oil for frying
¼ cup margarine
GF chicken broth

Preheat oven to 375 degrees. Spray a cookie sheet or jellyroll pan with GF baking spray.

Combine salt, pepper, and flours in a medium shallow bowl. Combine baking soda and water in a second shallow bowl.

Heat a shallow skillet over medium-high heat. Add about 3 tablespoons canola oil.

Cut flank steaks into 4 pieces, dip in water mixture, then flour mixture; fry in hot oil 3 minutes each side; drain. Transfer steak pieces to the prepared cookie sheet and place in preheated oven. Repeat until all meat has been fried and placed in the oven. Bake 10-15 minutes or until done.

Add any remaining flour to the pan along with ¼ cup margarine. Gradually add broth, scraping the pan drippings from the bottom of the pan. Bring broth to a boil, stirring constantly, until gravy is thickened and smooth. Add salt and pepper to taste. Top steaks with gravy and serve immediately.

Serves 4

Beef Jerky

This recipe requires time, but is well worth it. Most store-bought jerky contains gluten, and the few that do not are usually expensive.

2 Top Round London Broil steaks, 1½" thick
¼ cup GF soy sauce
¼ cup GF Worcestershire sauce
1 teaspoon GF liquid smoke (optional)
½ teaspoon garlic powder
1 teaspoon onion powder
1 teaspoon coarse ground pepper

Cut meat into very thin strips. (Meat is easiest to slice thin when partially frozen, or ask your butcher to slice it for beef jerky, in a meat slicer.)

Combine all remaining ingredients in large zip-top bag; add sliced meat and marinate for at least 24 hours, turning periodically.

Drain marinade from meat, discarding marinade, and place strips in a single layer on lightly sprayed roasting rack that has a drip pan. (Drip pan may be lined with foil for easy clean-up.)

Bake at lowest setting of oven (about 170 degrees) for 5 to 8 hours, depending on thickness of meat, or until meat is dry but still pliable.

Store in airtight container at room temperature for 3 days, or store in the freezer for up to 3 months.

Veal Parmesan

1 small red bell pepper, finely chopped
1 medium onion, finely chopped
1 stalk celery, finely chopped
1 clove garlic, minced
4 tablespoons olive oil, divided
1 (28-ounce) can whole peeled tomatoes, undrained and chopped
1 cup GF chicken broth
1 tablespoon tomato paste
1 tablespoon chopped fresh parsley
1 teaspoon sugar
¾ teaspoon dried basil
½ teaspoon salt
¼ teaspoon pepper
4 veal cutlets, about 4 oz. each
1 large egg
¼ cup sorghum flour mix
¾ cup unseasoned GF breadcrumbs (I prefer Gillian's Foods)
2 tablespoons butter
1½ cups shredded Mozzarella cheese
¾ cups grated Parmesan cheese

Preheat oven to 350 degrees. Spray a 13 x 9-inch baking dish with GF baking spray.

In a medium saucepan, sauté bell pepper, onion, celery, and garlic in 1 tablespoon of olive oil over medium heat for 5 minutes. Stir in tomatoes, broth, tomato paste, parsley, sugar, basil, salt, and pepper. Cover and simmer over low heat for 20 minutes. Uncover pan and cook over medium heat, stirring frequently, until sauce is very thick, about 20 minutes longer.

Meanwhile, pound veal ¼" thick; pat dry. Beat the egg in a shallow bowl. Spread flour and breadcrumbs each on separate plates. Dip veal first in flour, then in egg, then in breadcrumbs. Heat butter in 2 tablespoons of remaining oil in a 12-inch skillet over medium heat. Add veal, cooking until light brown, turning once, 2-3 minutes per side. Remove veal from skillet and place in the prepared baking dish. Sprinkle Mozzarella over veal, then spoon tomato sauce over cheese, and lastly, sprinkle Parmesan over tomato sauce. Drizzle remaining 1 tablespoon olive oil over parmesan. Bake uncovered until veal is tender and cheese is brown, about 25 minutes.

Authentic Italian Meatballs and Sauce

*This delicious recipe makes enough for a crowd,
or freeze in portions for several meals.*

Sauce:
4 cloves garlic, minced
1 large onion, chopped
1 sweet red bell pepper, chopped
½ teaspoon red pepper flakes
1 teaspoon salt
½ teaspoon pepper
¼ cup fresh chopped basil
1 (28-ounce) can crushed tomatoes
2 (28-ounce) cans tomato puree
1 (16-ounce) can tomato paste
2 tablespoons granulated sugar
1 cup white wine

Combine all ingredients in a large stock pot and bring to a boil. Reduce heat and simmer, covered, for up to 5 hours.

Meatballs:
2 pounds ground pork
2 pounds ground sirloin
3 eggs
1 teaspoon garlic powder
1 teaspoon salt
½ teaspoon pepper
1 cup dry GF breadcrumbs, or dried GF bread, broken into marble-
   size chunks
2 teaspoons oregano flakes

Preheat oven to 350 degrees.

Combine all ingredients in a large bowl or pot. Mix with hands until well combined. Form into golf ball size meatballs. Place on sprayed baking sheet and bake 20 minutes.

Remove meatballs from pan, add to sauce, stir gently, and simmer until sauce has completed its cooking time.

Yield: Makes 63 golf ball size meatballs

Apricot Habanero Short Ribs

Heat up your summer with Habaneros, some of the hottest peppers around. More delicate palates may choose to substitute jalapenos. Serve with potato salad for a perfect summer meal.

3 pounds beef short ribs
¼ cup onion, chopped
3 cloves garlic, minced
1 tablespoon canola oil
½ cup ketchup
½ cup apricot preserves
¼ cup cider vinegar
1 Habanero pepper, seeded and chopped
1 tablespoon Worcestershire sauce
1 teaspoon chili powder
½ teaspoon ground cumin
½ teaspoon salt

Trim fat from ribs. Place ribs in a 4 - 6 quart pot with enough water to cover ribs. Bring to boiling; reduce heat. Simmer, covered, for 1½ hours or until tender; drain.

For sauce, in a small saucepan cook the onion and garlic in hot oil until tender. Stir in the ketchup, apricot preserves, vinegar, pepper, steak sauce, and chili powder. Bring just to boiling; reduce heat. Simmer, uncovered, about 10 minutes or until mixture thickens slightly, stirring occasionally. Set aside.

Stir together the cumin and salt in a small mixing bowl. Sprinkle mixture evenly over both sides of the ribs; rub into surface.

Prepare grill for indirect grilling. Test for medium heat above the drip pan. Place ribs, meaty side up, on the lightly oiled grill rack over the drip pan. Cover and grill for 15 minutes or until the ribs are tender, brushing occasionally with the sauce. Heat the remaining sauce until bubbly; serve with the ribs.

Makes 6 servings

Orange Beef Stir-Fry

Light, quick, and easy, make this skillet dinner a good choice for any night of the week.

1 cup long-grain white rice, cooked
¼ cup freshly squeezed orange juice
1 tablespoon rice vinegar
1 tablespoon GF soy sauce
1 tablespoon packed light-brown sugar
1 pound top or bottom round steak, cut into strips, 2" long and ¼" thick
1 tablespoon cornstarch
Salt and pepper
1 bunch broccoli florets, broken into small pieces
2 tablespoons canola oil
1 red bell pepper cut into strips, 2" long and ¼" wide

In a small bowl combine orange juice, vinegar, soy sauce, and sugar; set aside. In a medium bowl, toss beef with cornstarch; season with salt and pepper, set aside.

In a large skillet, combine broccoli with 1 cup water; season with salt and pepper. Bring to a boil over medium-high heat and cook, partially covered, until broccoli is bright green and crisp-tender, 4 - 6 minutes. Transfer to a serving plate. Discard any water in skillet; wipe dry with a paper towel.

In same skillet, heat 1 tablespoon oil over high heat. When pan is hot, add half of the beef; cook until browned, 2 - 4 minutes. Using slotted spoon, transfer beef to the plate with the broccoli. Repeat with remaining oil and remaining beef.

Add orange-juice mixture and bell pepper to the skillet. Cook over high heat, stirring constantly until sauce thickens, 2 - 4 minutes. Return cooked beef and broccoli to skillet. Serve over hot cooked rice.

Serves 4

Cabernet Poached Flank Steak with Haricots Verts

*Cooking in a hot liquid, or poaching, is a very healthy way to cook.
This lean cut of beef, cooked in wine and herbs,
yields a tender steak with a rich flavor.*

1 pound flank steak
1½ cups cabernet wine
½ cup GF beef broth
2 cloves garlic, minced
1 small onion, cut into very thin rings
1 teaspoon dried oregano
½ teaspoon dried thyme
1 teaspoon pepper
1 bay leaf
2 teaspoons GF Dijon mustard (I prefer Annie's)
1 pound haricots verts

In a heavy bottomed, large sauté pan, combine cabernet, broth, garlic, onion, herbs, and bay leaf. Bring mixture to a gentle simmer. Add beef and cook 5-8 minutes on each side, depending on preferred doneness. Transfer cooked steak to a platter and cover to keep warm while cooking beans.

Stir mustard into poaching liquid and add haricots verts; cook for 3 minutes or until beans are just tender. Transfer to platter. Bring liquid to a vigorous simmer to reduce poaching liquid by half, about 5 minutes. Meanwhile, transfer beef to a cutting board and slice very thinly, against the grain.

To serve, divide haricots verts among four plates and top with thinly sliced beef. Drizzle with a bit of the reduced hot poaching liquid. Garnish with a few of the poached onion rings, and pepper.

Serves 4

Mojo-Marinated & Grilled Flank Steak

Mojos are boldly seasoned Latin American vinaigrette-type sauces. This one is good served with chicken as well as with flank steak. Thick slices of grilled Bermuda onion make a great accompaniment. Be sure to wear rubber gloves when handling hot Habaneros.

For the sauce:
4 tablespoons minced garlic (about 8-10 large cloves)
2 Habaneros or other spicy chiles, cored, seeded, and minced
4 teaspoons ground cumin seeds
1 cup olive oil
½ cup fresh lime juice
½ cup fresh orange juice
1½ tablespoons sherry vinegar
Salt and pepper

For the Steak:
1 (1½ pound) flank steak
Salt and pepper

Make the Mojo:
Place the raw garlic, chiles, cumin, and 1 teaspoon salt in a food processor fitted with the knife blade, pulsing until the ingredients are finely chopped but not pureed. Scrape the mixture into a bowl and set aside. Heat the olive oil until fairly hot, but not smoking, and pour it over the garlic-chili mixture (the oil should sizzle when it hits the cool ingredients), stir, and let stand for 10 minutes. This will cook the garlic slightly. Whisk in the lime juice, orange juice, and vinegar. Season with salt and pepper and set aside to cool completely. Put the steak in a zip-top bag or a shallow bowl and pour in a 1 cup of the cooled Mojo. Seal and refrigerate for at least 2 hours or overnight, turning occasionally. Refrigerate the remaining 1 cup of Mojo.

Cook and Serve:
Light a charcoal or gas grill. When the grill is hot, remove the steak from the marinade, discard marinade, pat dry, and season with salt and pepper. Grill for 5 - 7 minutes on one side and 3-4 minutes on the second side for medium rare. Remove from the grill and let rest for 5 minutes. Meanwhile, warm the reserved Mojo over low heat. Slice the flank steak very thinly on the bias and serve with the grilled onions and the reserved Mojo.

Wine Balsamic
Glazed Steak

Delicious and easy, this lean cut of steak cooks up tender when sliced thin and seared. Searing is a method of cooking where meat is cooked quickly using high heat, causing the natural sugar on the meat's surface to crystallize, locking-in its natural juices and allowing the meat to pull away from the pan and turn easily. It also browns the proteins in the meat which provides rich color and adds to the flavor. It is a healthy way to cook as very little fat is necessary. No fat is required if you are using a cast iron skillet. Meats can also be seasoned before searing; the seasoning will stick to the moist surface of the meat and form a flavorful crust as it cooks.

2 teaspoons vegetable or canola
2 pounds boneless top sirloin steak, sliced very thin against the
    grain (steaks are easiest to slice thin when partially frozen)
3 cloves garlic, minced
¼ teaspoon crushed red pepper
¾ cup dry red wine
2 cups sliced fresh mushrooms
3 tablespoons balsamic vinegar
2 tablespoons GF soy sauce
4 teaspoons honey
2 tablespoons butter (optional)

Heat the oil in a large heavy skillet over medium-high heat until very hot. When the oil ripples, the pan is hot enough to add the meat. (If the pan is not hot enough, the meat will stick to the pan and tear when turned). Add steak. Do not cover skillet. Reduce heat to medium, cook 10 - 13 minutes or to desired doneness, turning meat after 6-7 minutes. Transfer meat to platter and cover to keep warm.

Add the garlic and pepper to the hot skillet; cook 10 seconds. Remove skillet from heat and carefully add wine. Return to heat; bring mixture to a boil, uncovered, about 5 minutes or until most of the liquid is evaporated. Add mushrooms, vinegar, soy sauce, and honey; return to simmer. Cook and stir about 4 minutes or until mushrooms are tender. Add butter and stir until melted; spoon over steak.

Serves 5 -6

Pork

Crispy Apricot Pork Chops

1 tablespoon olive oil, plus more for the baking sheet
3 slices hard, dried GF sandwich bread
6 boneless breakfast pork chops (about ½-inch thick)
Salt and pepper
6 tablespoons apricot jam

Preheat oven to 425 degrees.

Lightly brush a rimmed baking sheet with oil.

Place bread in a food processor fitted with knife blade. Pulse until large crumbs form. Drizzle with oil; pulse once or twice, just until crumbs are moistened (you should have about 2½ cups crumbs.)

Season pork chops generously with salt and pepper. Spread one side of each chop with 1 tablespoon jam. Dividing evenly, sprinkle bread crumbs over jam and pat them on gently.

Transfer pork, coated side up, to prepared baking sheet. Bake until crust is golden and pork is opaque throughout, about 14 - 16 minutes (meat should register 150 degrees on an instant-read thermometer). Serve immediately.

Serves 6

Sweet and Sour Pork Skillet

A delicious recipe that also works well with beef and is best served over steaming rice.

2½ pounds pork loin, cubed
3 cups cooked rice
1 red bell pepper, chopped
1 green bell pepper, chopped
Fresh broccoli florets
2 purple onions, chopped
4 tablespoons olive oil, divided
Potato starch (not potato flour)

Marinade:
½ cup orange juice concentrate
3 tablespoons rice wine vinegar
Minced garlic
½ teaspoon ground ginger
½ teaspoon garlic powder

Sauce:
3 tablespoons rice wine vinegar
¼ cup packed brown sugar
½ cup orange juice concentrate
1 tablespoon GF soy sauce
Fresh cilantro, chopped
½ teaspoon ginger
1 tablespoon cornstarch

Prepare marinade in a gallon size zip-top bag. Add pork and marinate, refrigerated, at least 30 minutes. Drain pork, discarding marinade. Roll pork in potato starch. (Note: When I substitute beef in this recipe, I do not roll the beef in potato starch. Beef has a better texture if sliced thin and stir-fried without the starch coating.)

In a large saucepan cook peppers, broccoli, and onions in 1 tablespoon olive oil over medium-high heat until crisp-tender; season with salt and pepper. Transfer to a bowl.

Prepare sauce in a small bowl; set aside.

In saucepan over medium-high heat, fry pork in remaining 3 tablespoons olive oil. Reduce heat, cooking until done. Add veggies and sauce, stirring well. Serve immediately.

Fiery Asian-Style Pork Loin Roast

½ cup fresh orange juice
2 tablespoons frozen orange juice concentrate
2 tablespoons honey
1 tablespoon GF soy sauce
1 tablespoon olive oil
1 teaspoon minced garlic
1 teaspoon minced fresh ginger
½ teaspoon Chinese five-spice powder
2 drops hot chili oil
1 (4-pound) boneless pork-loin roast, trimmed

Combine orange juice, juice concentrate, honey, soy sauce, olive oil, garlic, ginger, five-spice powder, and chili oil in a gallon size zip-top bag. Knead the bag gently to combine the ingredients. Add the roast, zip the bag shut, and place bag in a shallow dish. Refrigerate for at least 2 hours or up to 24 hours.

Prepare a charcoal or gas grill, arranging the coals for indirect cooking. Lightly spray the grill rack with vegetable oil cooking spray. The coals should be moderately hot.

Lift the roast from the marinade, reserving the marinade for brushing it on the roast, two or three times during the first 30 minutes of cooking. Grill over indirect heat with the grill covered for about 1 hour and 10 minutes, or until a meat thermometer inserted in the center of the roast registers 150 degrees to 155 degrees. Remove the roast from the grill, and let it rest for about 10 minutes before slicing.

Yield: 4-6 servings

Pulled Pork

¾ cup GF ketchup
1 tablespoon packed brown sugar
3 garlic cloves, minced
¾ teaspoon dried sage
½ teaspoon dried oregano
Salt and pepper
3 pound boneless pork shoulder, trimmed of excess fat

In a 5-6 quart slow-cooker, stir together ½ cup ketchup, brown sugar, garlic, sage, oregano, 1 teaspoon salt and ½ teaspoon pepper. Cut pork in half and add each half to the slow cooker, turning to coat. Cover, and cook on lowest setting until meat is very tender and falling apart, about 8 hours.

Transfer pork to a large bowl. Using a large spoon, skim off and discard any fat from surface of cooking liquid. With two forks, pull meat apart until shredded. Add ¼ cup ketchup to juices from the slow cooker, stir to combine, and pour over pork. Season with salt and pepper to taste.

Cornbread and Sausage Stuffing

...a dressing with excellent flavor.

1½ pounds ground pork
1 large onion
3 stalks celery, finely chopped
Salt and pepper
2 pounds prepared GF cornbread, cut into ¾ inch cubes, and dried
2 - 3 tablespoons dried sage
2 - 3 large eggs
1- 2 cups reduced sodium GF chicken broth

Preheat oven to 350 degrees.

In a large skillet, cook sausage over medium heat, stirring often, until browned and cooked through, 5 - 8 minutes. With a slotted spoon, transfer to a large bowl.

To the skillet add onion, celery, and ¼ cup water. Stir vegetables, scraping up browned bits until vegetables soften, about 10 minutes. Season generously with salt and pepper; add to sausage.

Add cornbread, sage, and eggs to sausage and vegetables. Bring broth to a simmer in a small saucepan, pour ½ cup over stuffing, and toss gently (cornbread will break down into smaller pieces). If needed, add up to ½ cup more broth, until stuffing feels moist, but not wet. Stuff about 4 cups of dressing into the turkey. Cook according to the weight of the turkey (see directions on turkey packaging). Place any remaining stuffing in a sprayed baking pan and bake 1-2 hours, stirring every 20 minutes.

If you are not stuffing a turkey:
Pour all broth over the entire amount of stuffing, stirring well, and transfer to a sprayed 13 x 9-inch baking pan. Bake 1½ -2 hours, stirring every 20 minutes.

Sausage-Rice Pilaf

This tasty dish can be served as a side dish, complete meal,
or stuffed into an acorn squash, topped with cheese, and baked.
It also makes a colorful rice dressing for a holiday meal.

1 tablespoon olive oil
1 small sweet onion, chopped
2 cloves garlic, minced
2 stalks celery, chopped
1 cup petite frozen green peas, thawed
2 large organic carrots, chopped
1-pound fully cooked link sausage, cut into bite-size pieces
2 tablespoons dried cranberries, chopped
¾ teaspoon sage
¾ teaspoon thyme
½ cup chopped pecans
1 to 1½ cups cooked long-grain brown rice
Salt to taste

Preheat oven to 350 degrees.

In a large skillet sprayed with GF baking spray add olive oil and onion; sauté over medium heat until clear. Add garlic and celery and sauté 1 to 2 minutes more. Add peas, carrots, and sausage; cover and cook 3 minutes.

Add cranberries, sage, thyme, chopped pecans, and ½ teaspoon salt. Add cooked rice and mix well. Add salt to taste.

Stuffed acorn squash variation:
Cut each of 3 acorn squashes in half crosswise. Scoop out and discard seeds and strings. If necessary, trim the bottom so that the squash sits level, and place on a rimmed baking sheet with open end up. Sprinkle with ¼ teaspoon salt and ½ teaspoon nutmeg.

Cover pan with foil and bake the squash just until moist and tender about 45 - 50 minutes. Stuff each squash half with rice pilaf, top with grated mozzarella or crumbled feta cheese, and return to a 350 degree oven for 5 minutes. Serve immediately.

Serves 6

Sausage Kabobs

Prepare this meal in minutes under the broiler or on top of the grill.

1 pound GF sausage, cut into 24 pieces
2 small zucchinis, halved and cut into ½-inch pieces
½ large green bell pepper, cubed
1 medium crookneck yellow squash, cubed
Chunks of canned pineapple
6 tablespoons olive oil
3½ teaspoons GF Dijon mustard
1 teaspoon fresh lemon juice
1 teaspoon GF soy sauce
Salt and pepper to taste

Preheat grill or broiler to medium-high.

Soak 8, 12-inch wooden skewers in water for 2 minutes. Thread skewers alternating sausage, vegetables, and pineapple.

Combine olive oil and remaining ingredients in a small bowl; whisk well.

Place skewers on foil-lined baking sheet, or grill grate. Brush with half of the sauce. Place on grill or under broiler and cook 5 minutes. Turn skewers and brush sausage and vegetables with remaining sauce. Cook until browned, about 4-5 minutes more.

Serves 4

Pork-n-Beans

A must-try recipe, these spicy baked beans will heat up a cold day and are hearty enough to be a meal! This recipe allows you to get a head-start with canned beans and store bought barbeque sauce.

1 pound ground pork
1 onion, chopped
1 (28-ounce) can baked beans (I use Bush's Vegetarian)
2 (15-ounce) cans northern beans, drained
1 cup GF barbeque sauce (my favorite is Cattleman's Classic)
¼ cup GF spicy brown mustard
1 teaspoon pepper
½ teaspoon ground red pepper
1 teaspoon garlic powder
3 tablespoons molasses

Preheat oven to 350 degrees.

Brown pork in a skillet over med-high heat; drain on paper towels.

Combine sausage with remaining ingredients in a Dutch oven and bake 45 minutes. Or, add cooked sausage and remaining ingredients to a slow-cooker and cook 6 hours on lowest setting.

Serves 8

Baked Ham
with Orange-Honey Glaze

The perfect ham for a special meal…

1 (6-ounce) can frozen orange juice concentrate, thawed and
    undiluted
1¾ cups water
½ cup honey
3 tablespoons cornstarch
1 teaspoon dry mustard
½ teaspoon salt
½ teaspoon ground nutmeg
1 (3-inch) cinnamon stick
1 (7 - 9 pound) smoked, fully cooked, whole boneless ham
Whole cloves
2 oranges, peeled and sectioned

Combine first three ingredients in a medium saucepan. Remove ¼ cup of the mixture and combine with cornstarch, stirring until smooth. Add the cornstarch mixture back to the orange juice mixture in the saucepan, stirring until smooth. Add the mustard and next three ingredients. Cook over medium heat, stirring constantly, until mixture comes to a boil; cook 1 minute. Remove mixture from the heat and set aside.

Score fat on ham in a diamond design, and stud with cloves. Place ham, fat side up, on a rack in a shallow roasting pan. Insert meat thermometer, making sure it does not touch fat. Bake, uncovered, at 325 degrees for 2 hours or until meat thermometer registers 140 degrees.

After the first hour, baste the ham every 15 minutes with orange-honey sauce. Heat remaining sauce; add orange sections, and serve with ham.

Yield: 20-24 servings

Seafood

Gulf Coast Jambalaya

This fabulous recipe comes from southern Louisiana and makes enough for a crowd. If you are not serving a crowd it is good to know that the leftovers freeze very well! A cast iron Dutch oven works beautifully for this recipe as it goes from stovetop to oven with ease.

¼ cup olive oil
1 large onion, chopped
6 green onions, chopped
4 cloves garlic, minced
1 large green bell pepper, chopped
1 large red bell pepper, chopped
6 stalks celery, finely chopped
8 ripe tomatoes, chopped or 1 (28-ounce) can crushed tomatoes
1-pound cooked link sausage, chopped into bite-sized pieces
2 tablespoons dried oregano
4 teaspoons dried basil
2 teaspoons thyme
3 bay leaves
2 teaspoons cumin
1 - 2 teaspoons cayenne powder
3 cups GF chicken broth
3 cups uncooked white rice
1 pound shrimp, peeled, deveined, and cut into bite-size pieces
8 ounces fresh crabmeat, shell and cartilage removed
2 - 4 tablespoons chopped fresh cilantro
Salt to taste

Preheat oven to 350 degrees.

In a large cast iron Dutch oven or stock pot, heat olive oil over medium heat. Add onion and sauté. Add green onions, garlic, bell peppers, and celery; sauté 5 minutes more. Add tomatoes, sausage, and seasonings. Stir in chicken broth and bring to a boil on the stove top; jambalaya will be soupy. Add rice, stir well, cover and bake in preheated oven until rice is just tender, about 20 minutes, adjusting oven racks to accommodate the large pot.

Remove pot from the oven. (Liquids should have absorbed so jambalaya is no longer soupy.) Stir in shrimp, crabmeat, and cilantro. Cover and bake 10 - 15 minutes longer. Remove bay leaves. Taste, and adjust seasonings.

Serves 12

Individual Seafood Casseroles

2½ cups water
1 pound unpeeled fresh shrimp
1 cup fresh crabmeat, drained and flaked
1 cup thinly sliced celery
½ cup chopped pecans
½ cup mayonnaise
3 tablespoons grated onion
1 tablespoon lemon juice
1 tablespoon Worcestershire sauce
½ teaspoon salt
¼ teaspoon pepper
½ cup GF breadcrumbs (I prefer Gillian's Foods plain breadcrumbs)
Celery leaves

Preheat oven to 350 degrees. Spray 4 baking shells with GF baking spray.

Bring water to a boil; add shrimp, and return to a boil. Reduce heat, and simmer 3 minutes. Drain well; rinse with cold water; chill. Peel and devein shrimp. Set aside 4 shrimp for garnish.

Combine all ingredients except breadcrumbs, celery leaves, and shrimp for garnish.   Spoon mixture into prepared shells. Sprinkle with breadcrumbs. Bake 20 minutes or until heated through. Garnish with celery leaves and reserved shrimp.

Yield: 4 servings

Crispy Breaded Tilapia

Serve this excellent recipe with Classic Tartar Sauce, page 269.
See photo of Crispy Breaded Tilapia on the back cover.

½ cup sorghum flour mix
2 large eggs
2 cups plain breadcrumbs (I prefer Gillian's Foods breadcrumbs)
½ teaspoon salt
½ teaspoon pepper
4 skinless tilapia fillets (about 4-ounces each)
Vegetable or canola oil for the pan
1 large lemon, cut into wedges

Position a rack in the center of the oven and heat the oven to 400 degrees. Spray a 13 x 9-inch baking dish with GF baking spray. Line a cookie sheet with paper towels and set aside. Pour vegetable or canola oil ¼ -inch deep in a skillet or deep stock pot. Heat over medium-high heat until the oil is hot but not smoking or until a breadcrumb sizzles and browns when dropped in the oil.

Line up three wide, shallow dishes. Put the flour in the first; beat the eggs lightly in the second; place the breadcrumbs in the third. Add the salt and pepper to the flour and combine well. Working with one fillet at a time, coat it with flour and shake off the excess. Then dip the fillet in the egg, followed by the breadcrumbs.

Fry the fillets in hot oil, in batches, 2 to 3 minutes on each side; drain on paper towels. Place fillets in the prepared baking dish and transfer to the oven. Bake about 8 minutes.

Serve immediately with lemon wedges and tartar sauce.

Serves 4

Lemon Fish Cakes

This is a family favorite and one that kids love.

3 tablespoons olive oil
2 pounds tilapia fillets (about 5)
Salt and ground pepper
2 large eggs
½ cup GF mayonnaise
¼ cup chopped fresh parsley
¼ cup fresh lemon juice
½ cup GF oat bran (or GF oatmeal, processed in food processor)
1 cup GF cornflake crumbs

Preheat oven to 400 degrees.

Brush a 13 x 9-inch glass baking dish with ½ tablespoon oil. Place fillets in the baking dish. Roast until cooked through, 10 - 15 minutes. Let cool completely; pat dry with paper towels.

With a fork, flake fish into small pieces. In a large bowl, combine eggs, mayonnaise, parsley, and lemon juice. Fold in fish and oat bran; season with salt and pepper. Place cornflake crumbs on a plate. Form 16 cakes, using about ¼ cup fish mixture for each. Gently dredge cakes in crumbs, pressing to help crumbs adhere.

In a large skillet over medium-high heat, heat 1 tablespoon oil. Place 4 cakes in the skillet; cook until golden brown, 4 - 6 minutes per side. Repeat with remaining tablespoon oil and remaining 4 cakes.

Serve with tartar sauce, if desired.

Serves 8

Crispy Oven-Fried Fish

Make this easy recipe again and again.
It works well with Catfish, Tilapia, or Cod.

1 cup low-fat buttermilk (or add 1 teaspoon vinegar to 1 cup milk)
4 (6-ounce) catfish, tilapia, or cod fillets
2½ teaspoons salt-free GF Creole seasoning, optional
3 cups GF cornflakes cereal, crushed
GF vegetable or olive oil cooking spray
Lemon wedges

Place 1 cup low-fat buttermilk in a large zip-top plastic freezer bag; add fish fillets, turning to coat; seal and chill 20 minutes, turning once.

Preheat oven to 425 degrees. Line a baking sheet with parchment paper.

Remove catfish fillets from buttermilk, discarding buttermilk. Sprinkle fillets evenly with seasoning and a slight bit of salt, if desired.

Place 3 cups crushed cornflakes in a shallow dish. Dredge catfish fillets in cornflakes, pressing cornflakes gently to each fillet. Place fillets on prepared baking sheet. Bake 30 - 35 minutes or until fish flakes with fork. Serve immediately with lemon wedges.

Serves 4

Non-dairy version: Eliminate buttermilk. Dredge catfish or tilapia pieces in cornflakes, place coated fillets on prepared baking sheet, and lightly spray them with GF olive oil baking spray. Bake as directed.

Easy Baked Fish Sticks

This recipe results in light crispy fish sticks without any egg or dairy.
Don't overlook that they are quick and easy!!

4 (6-ounce) tilapia, cod, or catfish fillets
¼ cup GF powdered egg replacer
¼ cup water
GF dried breadcrumbs (I prefer Gillian's Foods plain breadcrumbs)
Salt, pepper or dried herbs of choice

Preheat oven to 400 degrees. Spray a glass 13 x 9-inch casserole or a baking pan with GF baking spray.

Whisk egg replacer in ¼ cup of water in a medium bowl until foamy.

Pour about 1 cup of breadcrumbs on a plate. Add ½ teaspoon salt, ½ teaspoon pepper, or your choice of dried herbs and seasonings.

Slice fillets into sticks. Dip fish pieces into egg replacer mixture, then dredge in breadcrumbs. Place on prepared baking pan. Bake 30 minutes or until cooked through and slightly brown. Serve with dipping sauce, ketchup, or lemon wedges.

Yield: 4 servings

Baked White Fish
in Wine Sauce

8 slices bacon (I prefer Applewood smoked bacon)
1 medium onion, chopped
1 Poblano pepper, seeded and chopped
6 whitefish fillets, such as tilapia or cod
½ cup GF breadcrumbs (I prefer Gillian's Foods plain breadcrumbs)
1 (14.5-ounce) can fire roasted tomatoes, undrained
¼ cup white wine

Preheat oven to 375 degrees.

Spray a 13 x 9-inch baking dish with GF cooking spray.

In a large saucepan, fry bacon until crisp. Remove from pan and drain on paper towels. Crumble bacon and place in a medium bowl. Remove all but 1 tablespoon of bacon grease from pan. Sauté onion until clear in remaining bacon grease; add peppers and sauté 2 minutes more. Add onion and pepper to bacon. Add bread-crumbs to bacon mixture and toss to combine.

Brown fish in the pan drippings, 2 minutes on each side. Place fish in the prepared baking dish.

Add tomatoes and wine to the saucepan, scraping drippings from bottom of pan; bring to a boil. Pour the mixture evenly over the fish. Top fish with bacon/breadcrumb mixture. Bake 20 minutes or until fish flakes easily; serve immediately.

Serves 6

Blackened Trout Fillets

1 tablespoon paprika
1 teaspoon dried thyme
1 teaspoon dry mustard
¼ teaspoon cayenne pepper
1 teaspoon salt
¼ teaspoon pepper
4 trout fillets
2 teaspoons butter, divided

Mix paprika and next 5 ingredients in small bowl, stirring with a fork until well combined. Transfer spice mixture to a plate.

Rinse trout fillets and pat dry.

Heat a large cast iron skillet over high heat. Dredge flesh side of fillets in spice mixture and shake off excess. Place fish in a single layer on a clean plate. Melt 1 teaspoon butter in the preheated skillet, swirling to coat the bottom. Immediately place two fillets in the skillet, flesh side down, and cook for two minutes. Turn and continue to cook until skin is crispy and trout is firm to the touch, about 5 minutes. Repeat with remaining butter and trout fillets.

Serves 4

Coconut Shrimp

1½ cups dried flaked coconut
¾ cup GF breadcrumbs (I prefer Gillian Foods breadcrumbs)
2 large egg whites
1½ pounds shrimp, peeled and deveined
GF sweet and sour dipping sauce (optional)

Preheat oven to 425 degrees. Spray a 13 x 9-inch baking pan with GF baking spray. Combine coconut and breadcrumbs on a plate. Whisk egg whites in a shallow bowl. Dip shrimp in egg whites, then breadcrumb/coconut mixture; place in the prepared pan. Continue until all shrimp are breaded. Bake 20-25 minutes, or until the shrimp begin to brown. Serve with the dipping sauce.

Serves 4-5

Easy Oven-Baked Salmon

Prepare this low fat dish using a cast iron skillet which will sear the meat on the outside, while keeping it moist on the inside.

2 tablespoons fresh lime juice
2 teaspoons grated fresh ginger
One (1¼-pound) salmon fillet, skin removed
Coarse-grained salt
2 limes cut in wedges

Whisk together lime juice and ginger in a small bowl. Place salmon fillet in a shallow dish; season with salt. Pour marinade over salmon, turning fish over to distribute evenly. Cover with plastic wrap and let stand, refrigerated, 15 minutes to one hour.

Preheat oven to 450 degrees. Place a 9 or 10-inch cast iron skillet in oven to heat.

Remove hot cast iron skillet from oven and place fish in skillet. Cook for 10 - 15 minutes, turning once at the halfway point. Cooking time will vary depending on the thickness of your fillet. Salmon should flake easily but not be dry; serve immediately.

Serves 4

Salmon with Potato-Artichoke Hash

Easy, tasty, and low calorie!

8 small red new potatoes, scrubbed and sliced ¼ inch thick
1 (14-ounce) can artichoke hearts in water, drained and halved
1 tablespoon dried thyme
1 teaspoon olive oil
Salt and pepper
1 salmon fillet (1½ pounds), cut crosswise into 4 pieces
½ cup fresh parsley, chopped
1 tablespoon GF Dijon mustard
1 tablespoon white-wine vinegar

Preheat oven to 475 degrees. Line an 11 x 15 x 2 ¾-inch pan with foil and spray with GF baking spray.

In a gallon size zip-top bag, toss together potatoes, artichokes, thyme, ½ teaspoon olive oil, ½ teaspoon salt, and ¼ teaspoon pepper. Empty vegetables onto the prepared pan. Arrange vegetables around sides of pan.

Place salmon pieces, skin side down, in center of pan. Coat with remaining ½ teaspoon olive oil, and sprinkle all over with salt and pepper. Roast, turning the vegetables once, until lightly browned and tender and salmon is just cooked through, about 20 minutes.

Meanwhile, make the sauce. Stir together ½ teaspoon salt, a pinch pepper, parsley, mustard, vinegar, and 1 tablespoon water.

Gently separate salmon pieces and top each with parsley sauce.
Serve with vegetables.

Serves 4

Cedar Plank Salmon

2 cedar grilling planks
3 tablespoons fresh parsley, chopped
3 tablespoons fresh lemon juice
2 tablespoons olive oil
2 - 3 garlic cloves, minced
Salt and pepper
1 salmon fillet, about 2 pounds

Place cedar planks in water, weigh down, and soak at least 2 hours.

Sauté garlic in olive oil over low heat; add parsley, lemon juice, salt and pepper. Remove from heat. Set aside.

Grill soaked cedar planks, covered, over medium-high heat 2 minutes or until they begin to smoke. Oil skin side of salmon with olive oil and place skin side down, on cedar plank. Cook 30 minutes over medium heat, covered.

Remove from grill and spoon herb mixture over.

Serves 4 – 5

Meatless
Main Dishes

Vegetable Tacos

Mighty tasty, these tacos were gobbled-up by even the
" non-eggplant eaters" in our home.

For the filling:
1 medium eggplant, peeled and cut into small cubes
1½ teaspoons salt
6 tablespoons olive oil, divided
1 small onion, diced
2 celery stalks, chopped
1 red bell pepper, seeded and chopped
3 garlic cloves, minced
1 (14.5-ounce) can fire roasted tomatoes
3 teaspoons chili powder
2½ teaspoons cumin
¼ cup chopped fresh parsley
1 (16-ounce) can black beans, rinsed and drained

GF corn taco shells
Chopped lettuce
Shredded Cheddar cheese (substitute dairy-free cheese if desired)
Sour cream

Place the eggplant cubes in a colander, sprinkle with salt, and allow the eggplant to drain for one hour. Meanwhile, heat 3 tablespoons olive oil in a large skillet over medium heat. Add onion and sauté until clear. Add celery and red pepper and sauté 2-3 minutes more. Push veggies aside and add garlic, sautéing until fragrant, about 1 minute. Drain most of the juice from the tomatoes and add tomatoes, chili powder, cumin, parsley, and beans to veggies. Stir well.

In a separate skillet, add remaining 3 tablespoons of oil and sauté eggplant until almost tender. Add eggplant to veggies. Adjust seasonings.

Place about ½ cup taco filling in each taco shell. Top with shredded cheese, lettuce, and sour cream.

Variation:
Make a veggie taco salad substituting corn tortilla chips for the taco shells.

Yield: Makes 8 tacos

Black Bean and Spinach Enchiladas

Though meatless, this tasty dish will fill-up your hungry bunch!
See photo on insert page C.

2 tablespoons canola oil
1 medium onion, chopped
3 cloves garlic, chopped
1 jalapeno, seeded and chopped
4 teaspoons cumin
4 teaspoons dried oregano
¼ teaspoon cayenne powder
1 teaspoon salt
½ teaspoon pepper
3 (14-ounce) cans black beans, rinsed and drained
2 (16-ounce) packages frozen, chopped spinach, thawed
1 (28-ounce) can tomato puree, divided
1 pound Colby-jack cheese, grated
18 GF white corn tortillas
Fresh cilantro, chopped

Preheat oven to 350 degrees. Spray an 11 x 15-inch baking pan with GF baking spray.

In a large saucepan, sauté onion in canola oil over medium heat until onion is clear. Add garlic and sauté one minute longer. Add jalapeno pepper, seasonings, and black beans. Mash beans slightly with a potato masher.

Place spinach in a colander, squeezing excess liquid from spinach. Add spinach to bean mixture along with 1 cup of tomato puree. Stir well and bring the mixture to a simmer, stirring occasionally. Meanwhile, place remaining tomato puree in a shallow bowl. Dip a tortilla in tomato puree, allowing excess to drip off, and place on a plate. Repeat with remaining tortillas, stacking tortillas one on top of the other. Remove bean mixture from heat. Spoon about ½ cup of bean mixture onto top tortilla, sprinkle with cheese, roll up, and place in prepared pan; repeat with remaining tortillas. Spoon remaining tomato puree over tortillas; top with remaining cheese. Bake 20 - 30 minutes. Garnish with cilantro and serve with salsa.

Yield: 18 enchiladas

Black Bean Cakes with Chipotle Cream

...an excellent recipe with fabulous flavor! Cakes can be made ahead and frozen up to 3 weeks in advance. Just thaw, bake as directed, and prepare Chipotle Cream to serve alongside these tasty bean cakes.

1 red bell pepper, diced
½ cup sliced green onion
½ cup frozen corn kernels, thawed
4 garlic cloves, minced
6 teaspoons olive oil, divided
2 (15-ounce) cans black beans, rinsed and drained
1½ teaspoons ground cumin
½ teaspoon dried crushed red pepper
¼ teaspoon salt
¼ teaspoon pepper
1½ cups GF breadcrumbs, divided (I prefer Gillian's Foods plain
    breadcrumbs)
3 tablespoons fresh cilantro, chopped
2 tablespoons GF mayonnaise
1 large egg, beaten

Preheat oven to 350 degrees. Spray a 13 x 9-inch baking dish with GF baking spray.

Heat a large skillet over medium-high heat. Add first five ingredients and sauté five minutes or until vegetables are tender. Remove from heat.

Mash 1½ cups black beans in a large bowl. Stir in remaining black beans, red bell pepper mixture, cumin, and next 3 ingredients. Add ½ cup breadcrumbs, cilantro, mayonnaise, and egg, stirring until well blended. Shape mixture into 6 patties. Roll each patty in breadcrumbs. Heat 2 tablespoons canola oil in a large skillet. Brown patties in oil, about 2 minutes each side, then transfer patties to the prepared baking dish. Bake 20 minutes.

Meanwhile, prepare **Chipotle Cream:**
In a small bowl combine 3 tablespoons mayonnaise and ½ teaspoon chipotle seasoning. Refrigerate until needed.

Yield: Makes 6 patties

Chalupas

*This meatless meal is a favorite with my kids.
Cooking the beans in advance
allows you to prepare this meal in a snap!*

8 (6-inch) tostado shells (I use El Milagro brand)
Refried beans (see recipe below or try Amy's Organic Refried Beans)
Grated Cheddar cheese
Chopped lettuce
Jarred salsa or Salsa Fresca, page 268
Toppings of choice such as sour cream or guacamole

Preheat oven to 400 degrees.

Place tostado shells singly on a jellyroll pan. Spread each shell with desired amount of mashed or refried beans, then top with grated cheese. Place in preheated oven for about 3 - 4 minutes or until cheese is melted and edges of tostado shells begin to brown.

Remove shells to individual plates and top with shredded lettuce, salsa, sour cream, and guacamole.

To cook dried pinto beans:
Wash pinto beans in colander. Place beans in a large bowl. Add water until it is 1-inch above the beans. Allow beans to soak overnight.

Drain beans in a colander, discarding water. Place beans in a large pot and add water until the water level is 1-inch above the beans. Add 1 whole minced onion, several slices of chopped bacon, 2 teaspoons salt, and 1 teaspoon pepper. Bring to a boil, then reduce heat to low and simmer, covered, until beans are very tender. Remove bacon; adjust seasonings. Mash desired amount with potato masher. Remaining beans can be frozen in portions for future meals.

Serves 4

Crustless
Tomato-Ricotta Pie

Serve this delicious cross between a frittata and a quiche
for dinner or brunch.

1 (15-ounce) container part-skim ricotta cheese
3 large eggs
¼ cup freshly grated Romano cheese or Parmesan cheese
Salt and pepper
¼ cup low-fat milk
1 tablespoon cornstarch
½ cup loosely packed fresh basil leaves, chopped
½ cup loosely packed fresh mint leaves, chopped
2 medium ripe tomatoes, thinly sliced

Preheat oven to 375 degrees. Lightly coat the inside of a 10-inch cast iron skillet with olive oil.

In a large bowl, whisk ricotta, eggs, cheese, ½ teaspoon salt, and ¼ teaspoon pepper until blended.

In a measuring cup, stir milk and cornstarch until smooth; whisk into cheese mixture. Stir in basil and mint.

Pour mixture into the prepared skillet. Arrange tomatoes on top, overlapping slices if necessary. Bake pie 35 minutes or until lightly browned and set around the edge. Let stand 10 minutes before serving.

Rice Lasagna

Our family is divided on this one…half prefer traditional lasagna, made with GF lasagna noodles, and half prefer this recipe, made with rice.

1½ cups cooked rice
1 (32-ounce) jar spaghetti sauce
1 (16-ounce) carton small curd cottage cheese
1 (8-ounce) package Mozzarella cheese
¼ cup grated Parmesan cheese, plus more for topping
1 egg

Preheat oven to 350 degrees. Spray a 9 x 13-inch glass baking dish with GF baking spray.

In a bowl of a food processor, fitted with knife blade, combine three cheeses with egg; process until smooth.

Divide rice into two portions. Spread half of rice into prepared pan. Spread ½ of cheese mixture over rice for a second layer. Spread 2 cups sauce over the cheese. Then repeat with rice, followed by the cheese mixture, then sauce. Sprinkle with additional grated Parmesan cheese.

Bake 50 minutes, uncovered. Cover lightly and let dish set 10 minutes before serving.

Yield: One 13 x 9-inch pan

Quinoa Egg Bake
with Thyme and Garlic

Quinoa is used as a moist crust in this recipe. I prefer to make this dish when I have 1 to 1½ cups of leftover cooked quinoa. Quinoa is touted as a "super food" as it contains all eight of the essential amino acids.

1 teaspoon butter or margarine
1 to 1½ cups cooked quinoa
8 eggs
1¼ cups milk
1 tablespoon chopped garlic
1 teaspoon chopped thyme
½ teaspoon salt
½ teaspoon pepper
2 cups packed baby spinach, roughly chopped
1 cup finely shredded Romano or Parmesan cheese

Preheat oven to 350 degrees. Grease a 10-inch cast iron skillet with butter. Spread cooked quinoa evenly over bottom of skillet.

In a large bowl, whisk together eggs, milk, garlic, thyme, salt, and pepper. Stir in the spinach then pour mixture over the quinoa. Cover tightly with foil. Bake until just set, about 45 minutes. Remove foil and sprinkle top evenly with cheese. Return to oven and bake, uncovered, until golden brown and crisp, 10 to 15 minutes more. Set aside to let cool briefly, then slice and serve.

Serves 4 as a main dish, 6 as a side dish

To cook quinoa:
Put quinoa into a fine mesh strainer and rinse until cold running water runs clear; drain well.

Bring 2¼ cups water or broth to a boil. Add 1 cup rinsed and drained quinoa to boiling liquid, reduce heat to simmer and cover, cooking until all liquid has been absorbed and quinoa has rings around it. (Cook quinoa just as you would rice, using double the amount of liquid per quinoa. The cooking time for rice and quinoa is also about the same.)

Serves 6

Vegetables

Vegetable Bake

A healthy, delicious way to serve vegetables, Vegetable Bake can accommodate a variety of vegetables and demonstrates how cast iron can go from the stove-top to the oven with ease.

6 tablespoons olive oil, divided
1 large sweet onion, thinly sliced into rings
3 garlic cloves, minced
Salt and pepper
2 medium zucchini, unpeeled, very thinly sliced
1 yellow squash, unpeeled, very thinly sliced
2 plum tomatoes, very thinly sliced
¼ cup white wine
Dried oregano
Grated Parmesan cheese (optional)

Preheat oven to 375 degrees.

Heat 3 tablespoons olive oil in a cast iron skillet over medium heat. Add onion rings and sauté until clear. Spread onions evenly over bottom of pan. Sprinkle garlic evenly over onions. Arrange vegetables on onion in slightly overlapping circles, alternating zucchini, squash, and tomatoes. Top with wine, 1 tablespoon olive oil, oregano, salt, and pepper. Bake 30 minutes. Drizzle with remaining oil. Top with grated Parmesan cheese. Bake 15 minutes longer.

Variation: Layer one thinly-sliced eggplant with vegetables.

Makes one 12-inch skillet

Lemon-Roasted Artichoke Hearts

Frozen artichoke hearts make this a quick, yet elegant side dish.

1 pound frozen artichoke hearts, thawed
2 tablespoons olive oil
1 tablespoon sherry cooking wine
2 medium garlic cloves, minced
1 tablespoon fresh lemon juice
½ teaspoon salt
½ teaspoon pepper

Preheat oven to 425 degrees. Line a 13 x 9-inch baking dish with foil and spray lightly with gluten-free baking spray.

Open bag of artichokes at one end. Empty artichoke hearts into a colander to drain. Return artichokes to original bag along with remaining ingredients. Hold open end of bag closed with one hand, and knead bag with other, combining the ingredients. Empty the artichokes onto the prepared pan. Roast artichokes about 12 minutes or until edges of artichokes are slightly brown.

Serves 4

Italian Green Beans

7½ cups fresh green beans (about 2¼ pounds)
2 cups chopped peeled tomato
2 cloves garlic, minced
¼ cup chopped fresh oregano
½ teaspoon pepper
¾ cup GF chicken broth

Wash beans and remove strings; cut into 1½ inch pieces. Place in a Dutch oven; add remaining ingredients, and bring mixture to a boil. Cover, reduce heat, and simmer 15 minutes or until beans are tender. Season with salt if broth is unsalted.

Yield: 10 servings

Michael's Baked Beans

2 (15-ounce) cans GF pork and beans, drained
¾ cup barbeque sauce (I use Cattleman's Classic barbeque sauce)
1 Granny Smith apple, peeled and chopped or grated
1 medium onion, chopped
½ cup firmly packed light brown sugar
1 teaspoon ground cumin
½ teaspoon ground red pepper
2-3 bacon slices, halved

Stir together first 8 ingredients in a lightly greased 2-quart baking dish or Dutch oven; top with bacon. Bake at 350 for 1 hour.

Yield: 6-8 servings

Green Bean Casserole

Update this family classic with colorful vegetables and creamy cheese.

1-pound frozen green beans
½ of a large red bell pepper, chopped
4 Tablespoons olive oil, divided
2 Tablespoons GF soy sauce
1 medium sweet onion, sliced into rings
2 Tablespoons light brown sugar, packed
GF breadcrumbs
3-ounces cream cheese, softened
1-ounce goat cheese, softened (optional)

Preheat oven to 375 degrees.

Place green beans in a colander. Run hot water over beans; drain.

Place onion rings, 2 Tablespoons olive oil, and brown sugar in a large skillet. Sauté until tender, stirring frequently. Place breadcrumbs on a plate. Toss several onion rings at a time in breadcrumbs to coat. Set aside.

Place green beans and bell pepper in a plastic bag with 2 tablespoons olive oil and soy sauce. Knead bag to thoroughly coat vegetables with oil. Spread vegetables onto a baking sheet sprayed with GF baking spray and roast for 15 minutes. Remove beans from oven and increase oven temperature to 400 degrees.

Combine softened cheeses and roasted beans and peppers in a bowl, stirring well. Spoon cheese/bean mixture into a casserole sprayed with GF baking spray. Top beans with onion rings and bake 6-8 minutes. Serve immediately.

Option: Add fresh sliced mushrooms.

Serves 4

Note: To serve 10-12 people use 2-pounds green beans, 1 large onion, 1 whole red bell pepper, and 6-ounces cream cheese.

Chinese Broccoli

1 pound Chinese broccoli, trimmed
2 tablespoons unsalted butter
2 teaspoons GF soy sauce
¼ teaspoon Chinese five-spice powder
¼ cup roasted soy nuts or peanuts, crushed

Steam the broccoli in a shallow skillet with 2 inches of water, until the stems are just tender, about 4-5 minutes. Transfer to a platter with a slotted spoon. Discard the water.

Combine the butter, soy sauce, five-spice powder, and 2 teaspoons water in the same skillet and heat over medium-low heat. Stir until the butter has melted. Return the vegetables to the skillet and toss until well combined. Top with the nuts, and serve immediately.

Makes 4 servings

Broccoli Stir-Fry

2 – 3 tablespoons extra virgin coconut oil
1 tablespoon minced garlic
1 bunch green onion, chopped
2 pounds boneless top sirloin steak sliced very thin
2 tablespoon GF soy sauce
1 bunch broccoli, chopped
2 large handfuls fresh spinach
2 drops dark sesame oil
1 tablespoon fresh ginger, grated

Heat wok or skillet to medium high; add coconut oil, garlic, onion, sliced beef, and soy sauce. Cook until beef is almost done, stirring constantly. Add broccoli, spinach, sesame oil, and fresh ginger. Stir for 1 minute. Serve immediately.

Serves 4 - 5

Spaghetti Squash Sauté

1 (2½ pound) spaghetti squash
1 tablespoon chopped fresh oregano
4 ripe tomatoes, quartered
1 bunch green onions, chopped
2 garlic cloves, minced
1 teaspoon olive oil
¼ cup dry white wine
1 teaspoon salt
½ teaspoon freshly ground pepper
¼ cup shaved Parmesan cheese, optional

Preheat oven to 450 degrees.

Cut squash in half lengthwise, and place, cut side down, in a foil-lined 15 x 10-inch jellyroll pan. Bake for 30 minutes or until skin is tender and strands may be loosened easily with a fork. Remove seeds. Cool squash slightly. Remove spaghetti-like strands with a fork, discarding shells.

Sauté chopped oregano and next 3 ingredients in hot oil in a large skillet for 2 minutes. Stir in wine, salt, and pepper, and cook for 2 minutes more. Remove from heat; stir in squash. Sprinkle with cheese; serve immediately.

Yield: 4 servings

Stuffed Pablano Peppers

3 garlic cloves, minced
2 stalks celery, chopped
1 green bell pepper, chopped
1 tablespoon olive oil
4 plum tomatoes, chopped
1 cup frozen corn, thawed
Chopped fresh cilantro
3 medium Poblano peppers, halved and seeded
Monterrey jack cheese, grated

Preheat oven to 350 degrees.

In a large saucepan, sauté garlic, celery, and bell pepper in olive oil until fragrant, about 2 minutes. Add tomatoes, corn and cilantro; stirring well.

Place halved Poblano peppers on foil-lined baking sheet, cut side up. Fill peppers with mixture; bake 30 minutes. Remove pan from the oven, top peppers with cheese, and return to the oven to bake 10 minutes longer.

Variation:
Top the vegetables with Salsa Fresca, page268, before topping with cheese and baking the final 10 minutes.

Serves 6

Okra Étouffée

Take advantage of fresh okra during its peak season and perk up leftover grilled chicken or meat loaf with this mouthwatering side dish.

3 cups sliced fresh okra
2 tablespoons olive oil
1 (10-ounce) can diced tomatoes and green chiles, undrained
1 medium onion, chopped
1 medium-size green bell pepper, chopped
¾ teaspoon salt
¼ teaspoon pepper
¾ cup crushed GF potato chips
¼ cup plain GF breadcrumbs or dry GF bread, crumbled

Place okra in a lightly sprayed 1½ quart baking dish or a Dutch oven; drizzle with oil.

Top okra with tomatoes and green chiles, onion, and bell pepper; sprinkle with salt and pepper. Cover loosely with aluminum foil or place lid on a Dutch oven.

Bake 400 degrees, stirring occasionally, for 1 hour. Stir together crushed potato chips and breadcrumbs; sprinkle over casserole and bake uncovered, 15 minutes longer. Serve over rice, if desired.

Yield: 6 servings

Fast and Fabulous Pickles

Nothing beats homemade pickles but the work of traditional canning methods leaves a lot to be desired. This new-fashioned recipe is tailored for busy cooks and results in terrific pickles every time. Be sure to use pickling cucumbers, and freezer space is required.

3½ cups thinly sliced pickling cucumbers (about 1 pound)
1 medium sweet onion, sliced and separated into rings
2 jalapeno peppers, seeded and sliced
3 large cloves garlic, minced
1 tablespoon salt
1 cup granulated sugar
1 cup white vinegar (5% acidity)
2 tablespoons water

Combine first 5 ingredients in a large bowl.

Cook 1 cup sugar, 1 cup vinegar, and 2 tablespoons water in a saucepan over medium heat, stirring until sugar dissolves. Pour mixture over cucumber mixture. Cover tightly with plastic wrap and chill 48 hours.

After cucumbers have chilled, spoon evenly into 6 half-pint or 3 pint-size canning jars, leaving ½-inch of room at the top; seal, label, and freeze pickles 8 hours or up to 6 months. Thaw in refrigerator before serving; use thawed pickles within 2 weeks.

Makes about 3 pints

Onion Rings

The sweet onions of summer tempt me to get out the fryer for these crisp onion rings with a light batter.

2 large onions, preferably Vidalia or Spanish, cut into ¼ inch rings
Vegetable oil or canola oil for frying
1¼ cups sorghum flour mix
½ cup cornstarch
1 tablespoon baking powder
1½ teaspoons salt
1 tablespoon honey
Ketchup or ranch dressing for dipping

In a large bowl of cold water, soak the onion rings for 10-15 minutes; drain on paper towels.

Meanwhile, in a large deep pot, heat 2-inches of oil over medium-high heat until it registers 360 degrees on a deep-fat thermometer. Fill a large bowl halfway with ice. In a medium bowl, whisk the flour mix, cornstarch, baking powder, salt, and honey. Add the ice water and stir just until a batter forms. (The batter will be thin, with small lumps and bubbles.) Place the batter bowl inside the bowl of ice to keep cold.

Using tongs, coat the onion rings with the batter, letting the excess drip off. Working in batches, drop the rings into the oil and fry until light golden, 2½ to 3 minutes. Using the tongs, transfer the rings to paper towels to drain, returning the oil to 360 degrees between batches. Serve with dipping sauces or ketchup.

Deviled Potatoes

This is one of my daughter's favorite recipes,
and an easy recipe for young people who are learning to cook!

5 medium baking potatoes
1 teaspoon salt
4 tablespoons softened butter
½ cup warm milk
¾ cup sour cream
2 tablespoons GF prepared mustard
1 tablespoon granulated sugar
4 tablespoons chopped green onions

Preheat oven to 350 degrees. Spray a 1-quart casserole with GF baking spray.

Fill a large stock pot half-full with water and bring to a boil. Cut washed, peeled potatoes into fourths and add to the boiling water along with the salt. Partially cover the pot with the lid, and cook until tender when tested with a fork; drain.

Return potatoes to the hot pot and add butter and milk, mashing until free of lumps. Add remaining ingredients and stir until well combined. Transfer the potato mixture to the prepared casserole.
Bake 12 minutes.

Serves 5 -6

Lemon Fingerling Potatoes

1 pound fingerling potatoes
1 tablespoon plus ½ teaspoon coarse salt
1 tablespoon olive oil
1 garlic clove, minced
¼ cup GF chicken broth
2 tablespoons dry white wine
1 tablespoon dry thyme
1 tablespoon butter
2 tablespoons fresh lemon juice
Pepper to taste

Cover potatoes with water in a shallow pan. Add 1 tablespoon salt, and bring to a boil. Reduce heat, and simmer until tender, about 10 minutes. Drain potatoes and halve lengthwise.

Heat oil in a large skillet over medium heat. Add garlic, and cook until soft, about 2 minutes. Add potatoes, cut sides down, and cook until golden brown, about 10 minutes.

Stir in broth, wine, and remaining ½ teaspoon salt. Cook until liquid is reduced by a third, about 2 minutes. Remove from heat. Add thyme and butter, and stir until butter has melted. Stir in lemon juice, salt, and pepper.

Serves 4

Southwest Twice-Baked Potatoes

2 pounds medium-size new potatoes
1 tablespoon olive oil
½ cup Cheddar cheese, shredded
2 tablespoons sour cream
1 tablespoon melted butter
2 tablespoons buttermilk
½ teaspoon pepper
½ teaspoon salt
1 (4.5-ounce) can diced green chiles, drained
Paprika for garnish

Cut a thin slice from the bottom of each potato to form a flat base; brush potatoes evenly with oil, and place on a baking sheet.

Bake at 350 degrees for 45 minutes or until tender. Remove from oven, and let cool slightly.

Cut a thin slice from the top of each potato. Carefully scoop out potato pulp into a mixing bowl, leaving shells intact. Add shredded Cheddar cheese and next 5 ingredients to the potato pulp and beat at medium speed with an electric mixer until smooth and creamy. Stir in green chiles. Spoon mixture evenly into each potato shell and place on a baking sheet.

Bake potatoes for 20 minutes or just until lightly browned. Garnish with paprika if desired.

Serves 6

Crisp Potato Skins

Serve these potato skins as a side dish, or reinvent them by adding pasta sauce, mozzarella, and diced pepperoni.

4 medium russet potatoes (I prefer organic russets for this recipe)
¼ cup olive oil
1 teaspoon salt
½ teaspoon pepper

Adjust oven racks to highest and middle positions. Preheat oven to 450 degrees.

Pierce each potato eight times with a fork. Place directly on middle oven rack, and bake until tender when pierced with a fork, about 40 minutes. Let stand until cool enough to handle.

Cut each potato in half lengthwise, and then cut each half lengthwise again, to make 16 wedges. Use a small spoon to scoop out inside of each wedge, leaving about ¼-inch shell all around. (Potato pulp can be reserved for mashed potatoes later in the week.)

Combine oil, salt, and pepper in a small bowl. Brush all sides of each wedge with the oil mixture. Place on baking sheet lined with foil. Bake on highest rack until crisp and edges are golden, about 20 minutes. Best served hot!

Serves 4

Cast Iron Hash Browns

Use a cast iron skillet to heat a ham steak
then remove ham and prepare this dish which uses frozen hash browns
for a quick one-skillet meal.

1 small green bell pepper
1 small red bell pepper
1 medium yellow onion
1 (1-pound, 14-ounce) bag frozen hash browns
¼ cup plus 2 tablespoons olive oil
Salt and pepper

Finely chop the bell peppers and onion   Heat a 10-inch cast iron skillet over medium-high heat. Add 2 tablespoons olive oil. Add peppers and onion and cook until onions are clear. Add thawed hash browns. Drizzle ¼ cup olive oil over potatoes, sprinkle with salt and pepper, and stir until well blended. Adjust seasonings.

Smooth potatoes evenly in pan and press down with back of spoon or egg-turner. Cook 2 - 3 minutes, turn, and cook 2 - 3 minutes more.

Serves 5-6

Potato Cakes

Essentially, these are seasoned mashed potatoes shaped into cakes and pan-fried until they've developed a delicious crusty exterior. Serve as a side dish or with bacon and eggs for brunch. Top with sour cream and chives if desired.

1 pound Yukon gold potatoes
Salt and freshly ground pepper
¼ cup packed finely grated Asiago cheese, optional
5 tablespoons olive oil, divided
3 tablespoons sour cream; more for serving
¼ cup thinly sliced fresh chives; more for serving

Place the potatoes and 1 teaspoon salt in a medium sauce pan and add water to cover by about ½-inch. Partially cover and bring to a boil over high heat. Boil until the potatoes are tender when pierced with a fork, 20-30 minutes; drain. Remove the peeling from potatoes when potatoes are cool enough to handle.

Pass potatoes through a ricer or food mill back into the saucepan (or mash them as smoothly as possible with a hand masher). Add the cheese, 3 tablespoons of the olive oil, sour cream, ½ teaspoon salt, and ¼ teaspoon pepper. Mix thoroughly. Add the chives and stir until well mixed. Season the potato mixture with extra salt and pepper, if necessary. Portion the potato mixture into quarters and shape each into a patty about ¾-inch thick.

Heat the remaining 2 tablespoons olive oil in a 10-inch non-stick skillet over medium-high heat. When the oil is hot, set the cakes in the pan so they aren't touching. Cook until a deep brown crust forms, 2-3 minutes, and then turn and brown the other side, another 2-3 minutes.

Yield: Four potato patties

Lemon-Glazed Sweet Potatoes

6 medium sweet potatoes (about 4 pounds)
¾ cup water
¼ cup granulated sugar
¼ cup light brown sugar, packed
½ teaspoon salt
3 tablespoons lemon juice
½ teaspoon nutmeg
3 tablespoons unsalted butter, divided

Preheat oven to 350 degrees.

Place potatoes in a large pot with enough water to cover potatoes; bring to a boil. Reduce heat, simmer 10 - 12 minutes or until potatoes are tender. (Potatoes should be tender on the outside but resistant in the center when pierced with the tip of a paring knife.) Drain potatoes; cool.

Meanwhile, in a nonreactive saucepan, combine the water, sugars, and salt; bring to a boil, stirring just until sugars are dissolved. Simmer 8 minutes; remove from heat. Stir in lemon juice, nutmeg, and 2 tablespoons butter.

Butter a large shallow glass baking dish with the remaining tablespoon of butter. Peel potatoes, cut crosswise into ¾-inch slices. Arrange slices in single layer in baking dish. Pour lemon syrup over. Bake in preheated oven 40 - 50 minutes, basting occasionally, until potatoes are well glazed and begin to caramelize on the edges.

Serves 6

Sweet Potato Casserole

This mouthwatering casserole is a great addition to a Thanksgiving feast!

4½ pounds sweet potatoes
½ cup granulated sugar
¼ cup milk
½ cup butter, softened
2 large eggs
1 teaspoon pure vanilla extract
¼ teaspoon salt
1¼ cups GF cornflake cereal, crushed
¼ cup chopped pecans (optional)
1 tablespoon packed brown sugar
1 tablespoon butter, melted
1½ cups GF miniature marshmallows

Preheat oven to 400 degrees. Spray an 11 x 7-inch baking dish with GF baking spray.

Bake sweet potatoes for about 1 hour or until tender. Peel and mash sweet potatoes.

Beat mashed sweet potatoes, sugar, and next 6 ingredients at medium speed with an electric mixer until smooth. Spoon potato mixture into the prepared baking dish.

Combine cornflakes cereal and next 3 ingredients in a small bowl; sprinkle diagonally over casserole in rows 2-inches apart.

Reduce oven to 350 degrees and bake for 30 minutes. Remove from oven; let stand 10 minutes. Sprinkle alternate rows with marshmallows and bake an additional 10 minutes. Let stand 10 minutes before serving.

Yield: 8 servings

Spinach Frittata

*Frittatas are easy because the fillings get whisked right into the eggs.
They are also versatile; change the filling and flavor to suit your mood.
And, they make a tasty breakfast or can be served with a salad or soup for
lunch or dinner.*

1 (10-ounce) package frozen spinach, thawed
8 large eggs
½ cup whole milk, half and half, or heavy cream
1 tablespoon sorghum flour mix
1 teaspoon salt
Fresh ground black pepper
1 large sweet onion, thinly sliced
½ large red bell pepper, diced
2 tablespoons olive oil; more as needed

Place spinach in a colander and squeeze excess liquid from spinach, reserving liquid for another use (such as soup).

Heat the oven to 350 degrees. In a large bowl, lightly whisk the eggs, milk or cream, flour mix (don't worry if small lumps form), salt, and several grinds of pepper.

Heat a 10-inch heavy skillet to medium-high and add onion and a little oil if needed; sauté onion until tender. Add the red pepper and sauté 2 minutes longer. Remove the onions and pepper from the pan.

Wipe the pan clean. Heat about 2 tablespoons olive oil over medium heat.

Fold the spinach, onions, and peppers into the egg mixture. Add the mixture to the hot skillet, spreading everything evenly. Reduce the heat to low, cover, and cook until the eggs are set about 1-inch in from the sides of the pan, 8 - 10 minutes. Uncover the pan and place in preheated oven. Cook until the top is puffed and completely set, 15 - 25 minutes longer.

Makes one 10-inch frittata

Variations:
Try omitting the spinach and adding cooked ham chunks with ½ cup cheddar cheese. Or, omit the spinach and red pepper and add chopped sundried tomatoes, fresh chopped basil, and oregano.

Spinach and Potato Skillet Bake

This can be a perfect side dish for a roast, chicken, or to serve with a cup of soup on a cold day.

2 tablespoons butter, divided
1 tablespoon extra virgin olive oil
½ medium yellow onion, finely chopped
3 cloves garlic, minced
5 medium baking potatoes
Salt and pepper to taste
1 bunch fresh spinach, washed, dried, and coarsely chopped
1 cup grated white cheese such as Swiss, or use a combination

Preheat oven to 350 degrees.

Heat 1 tablespoon of butter and the olive oil in a 10-inch cast iron skillet. Add the onion and cook over medium heat for five minutes or until onion is translucent. Add the garlic and sauté one minute longer. Remove skillet from heat and arrange a third of the potatoes in a single layer in the skillet over the onion and garlic. Sprinkle with salt and pepper and top with a third of the spinach leaves. Sprinkle a third of the grated cheese over the spinach. Repeat the layers two more times in the same way, ending with the cheese. Cut the remaining tablespoon of butter into small pieces and dot them over the cheese.

Cover tightly with aluminum foil and bake until the potatoes are easily pierced with the tip of a knife, 1¼ - 1½ hours. Slice into wedges.

Serves 4 to 6 people

Spinach Puffs

These yummy puffs work great as a side dish with ham, a bowl of tomato soup, or all by themselves!

2 packages frozen chopped spinach, thawed
1 cup sorghum flour (not mix)
½ cup tapioca starch
½ cup cornstarch
½ cup butter
1½ cups milk
1 teaspoon salt
4 eggs
8-ounces shredded Swiss cheese

Preheat oven to 375 degrees. Generously spray 24 muffin tins with GF baking spray.

Place spinach in a colander and squeeze out excess water.

Bring butter, milk, and salt to a boil in a medium saucepan, stirring constantly. Transfer liquid to a mixing bowl. Add flour and starches, mixing at low speed. Add eggs and beat on high for 3 minutes. Stir in spinach and cheese; spoon into prepared muffin tins.

Bake 23-28 minutes or until a tester comes out clean and puffs begin to brown. Serve warm.

Refrigerate leftovers. Puffs can be heated under the broiler until warm or in the microwave for 35 seconds.

Yield: Two dozen puffs

Rice
and
Quinoa

Snappy Side Dish Rice

Start with a can of diced tomatoes with green chilies for a quick, tasty side dish.

1 tablespoon olive oil
1 small onion, chopped
1 cup Basmati rice
1 (14.5-ounce) can diced tomatoes and green chiles in juice
2 teaspoons dried oregano
Salt and pepper

Heat oil in a skillet, add onion, sautéing until clear.

Stir in tomatoes and chiles with their juice, oregano, 1¼ cups water; season with salt and pepper.

Bring to a boil; reduce heat to medium-low, and simmer, tightly covered, until rice is tender, about 15 minutes. Remove from heat and let stand, covered, for 5 to 10 minutes. Fluff with fork before serving.

Serves: 5

Brown Rice Pilaf

Serve as a side dish, or toss-in leftover roasted chicken for a meal.

4 tablespoons olive oil
1 small yellow onion, chopped
2 cloves garlic, minced
1 teaspoon ground cumin
1 cup uncooked long-grain brown rice
2 cups water
½ teaspoon salt
¼ teaspoon freshly ground pepper
2 cups cherry tomatoes, halved
2 tablespoons fresh parsley, finely chopped
2 tablespoons fresh basil, finely chopped

Heat 2 tablespoons olive oil in a skillet over medium heat; add onion, cooking until onion is clear. Add garlic and cumin and cook 30 seconds. Add brown rice and cook over medium heat 3 - 4 minutes. Add water and stir to mix well. Add salt and pepper and bring rice mixture to a boil. Reduce heat, cover and simmer about 40 minutes or until all liquid has been absorbed.

Add tomatoes and herbs and stir gently until well combined.

Yield: 6 servings

Baked Almond Wild Rice

1 cup uncooked wild rice
2 tablespoons chopped onion
4 tablespoons slivered almonds
4 tablespoons butter or margarine, melted
3 cups boiling GF chicken or beef broth

Sauté rice, onion, and almonds in the butter 5 minutes or until almonds are browned. Stir in broth. Pour into an ungreased 13 x 9-inch casserole. Cover and bake at 350 degrees for 1 hour and 15 minutes.

Yield: 4 servings

Sundried Tomato Risotto

This yummy side dish compliments many meat dishes including pork chops, roasted chicken, roast beef, and seafood.

1 (4-ounce) jar sundried tomatoes packed in oil, drained
2¾ cups GF chicken broth
1 cup finely chopped onion
1 garlic clove, minced
2 tablespoons olive oil
1 cup uncooked Arborio rice
¼ cup freshly grated Parmesan cheese
Finely chopped fresh parsley leaves

Finely chop the sundried tomatoes.

In a saucepan bring the chicken broth to a simmer and keep it at a simmer.

In a large saucepan cook the onion and the garlic in the oil over moderately low heat, stirring, until they are softened. Add the rice, stirring until each grain is coated with oil. Stir in the tomatoes.

Add ½ cup of the simmering liquid and cook the mixture over moderate heat, stirring constantly, until the liquid is absorbed. Continue adding the liquid, ½ cup at a time, stirring constantly and letting each portion be absorbed before adding the next, until the rice is tender but still al dente. (The rice should take about 17 minutes to cook.)

Stir in the Parmesan cheese and season with salt and pepper to taste. Stir in the chopped parsley. Serve immediately.

Serves 4-5

Lemon Risotto

Risotto is Arborio Rice, cooked to a creamy texture.
Serve it as a side dish, or as a main course.

3 cups GF chicken broth
2 tablespoons butter
1½ tablespoons olive oil
1¼ cups chopped green onion
1 cup Arborio rice
2 tablespoons dry white wine or white cooking wine
½ cup grated Parmesan cheese, optional
1 tablespoon chopped fresh parsley
1 tablespoon fresh lemon juice

Bring broth to simmer in a large saucepan over medium heat. Reduce heat to low; cover to keep warm.

Melt butter with oil in a heavy large saucepan over medium heat. Add green onions and sauté until tender, about 5 minutes. Add rice; stir 1 minute. Add wine and stir until evaporated, about 30 seconds. Add 1½ cups hot broth; simmer until absorbed, stirring frequently. Add remaining broth ½ cup at a time, allowing broth to be absorbed before adding more, and stirring frequently until rice is creamy and tender, about 30 minutes. Stir in cheese, parsley, and lemon juice; season with salt and pepper, if desired. Serve immediately.

Serves 5-6

Quinoa Pilaf

Be sure to read about quinoa's powerful nutrition in the section Great Gluten-Free Grains, page 15. And remember, just about any rice recipe can be adapted to a quinoa recipe. The basic recipe for cooking quinoa is included in The Complete Book of Gluten-Free Cooking or use the simple directions below. Other great quinoa recipes can be found in the Salads section and in the section, Meatless Main Dishes. Check out the index for a complete list of recipes which incorporate quinoa.

¼ cup olive oil
2 cloves garlic, minced
½ cup shredded carrot
¼ cup chopped celery
½ cup diced green onion
¼ cup diced green pepper
¼ cup diced sweet red pepper
3 cups cooked quinoa (see cooking directions below)
1 cup sliced almonds
¼ teaspoon oregano
¼ teaspoon parsley
Salt to taste

Sauté garlic in olive oil until fragrant, about 1 minute. Add shredded carrots, celery, green onion, and peppers; sauté until heated, about 2 minutes longer. Combine cooked quinoa and remaining ingredients with veggies and stir to combine.

Serves 6 as a side dish

To cook quinoa:
Rinse quinoa in a fine mesh strainer under cold water; drain. Bring 3 cups water or broth, to a boil. Add 1½ cups quinoa, reduce to low, and simmer until liquid is absorbed and quinoa has visible "rings" around each grain.

Quinoa with a Kick

*Serve this quinoa as a side dish to accompany grilled meat
or serve it as a vegetarian main dish.*

1¼ cups quinoa, uncooked
2 cups water
1½ cups GF salsa
1 teaspoon cumin
½ teaspoon salt
½ teaspoon pepper
2 jalapeno peppers, seeded and chopped
1 - 2 cloves garlic, minced
1 tablespoon canola oil
1 (15-ounce) can black beans, rinsed and drained
1½ cups frozen corn, thawed
1 cup chopped tomatoes

Rinse quinoa in a fine mesh strainer under cold water to remove naturally occurring resin; drain. Place quinoa, water, salsa, cumin, salt, and pepper in large saucepan over high heat. Bring to a boil; reduce to simmer and cook until rings form around quinoa and all liquid is absorbed.

While quinoa is cooking, add jalapeno peppers and garlic to the oil in a medium skillet. Sauté 1-2 minutes, then add beans, corn, and tomatoes to skillet, stirring gently until warm.

Add bean/corn mixture to cooked quinoa, tossing to combine; serve immediately.

Serves 6 as a side dish

Rice and Peas

This creamy side dish works well with roast, pork chops, or a ham steak.

1 tablespoon olive oil
1 medium onion, chopped
¼ teaspoon salt
1½ cups brown rice
4 garlic cloves, minced
3 cups GF vegetable or chicken broth
1 red bell pepper, chopped
1 (16-ounce) package frozen peas
4 ounces cream cheese
½ cup grated Parmesan or Cheddar cheese

Heat oil in a skillet; add onion and salt. Cook until soft and just beginning to brown, 4 - 6 minutes, stirring often. Add rice and garlic and cook until the garlic is fragrant, 30 seconds to 1 minute. Add broth and bring to a boil. Cover, reduce heat, and simmer until rice is cooked.

Stir in peas and cream cheese until the mixture is creamy and the cheese is incorporated. Stir in Parmesan or Cheddar cheese and serve immediately.

Pasta

Vegetable Pasta

Simply yummy...add your own variations such as black olives, or cherry tomatoes, halved. See photo on cover and insert page A.

8-ounces GF fettuccini
¼ cup olive oil, divided
1½ cups zucchini, sliced thin, then cut in half for bite-size pieces
3 cloves garlic, minced
1 cup fresh basil leaves
1 teaspoon sage
1 teaspoon oregano
Salt to taste
1½ cups frozen artichoke quarters, thawed
Grated Parmesan cheese
Halved cherry tomatoes, optional

Allow artichoke hearts to come to room temperature.

Cook fettuccini, according to package instructions; drain.

Meanwhile, sauté zucchini in 2 tablespoons olive oil, until tender, about 4 - 5 minutes. Add garlic and sauté until fragrant, about 45 seconds; set aside.

Add remaining olive oil, basil, sage, and oregano to a food processor fitted with the knife blade; process until smooth.

Drain cooked pasta, then return pasta to the hot pot along with zucchini mixture, herb mixture, artichoke hearts, and grated Parmesan; toss well. Add black olives or halved cherry tomatoes if desired; season with salt to taste.

Serves 4-5 as a side dish, serves 2-3 as a main dish

Quick Penne Pasta
with Fire-Roasted Tomatoes

7 ounces GF brown rice Penne pasta
4-5 tablespoons olive oil
2 -3 cloves garlic, minced
1 (14.5-ounce) can fire roasted tomatoes
Dash of red pepper flakes
Salt and pepper
Splash of balsamic vinegar
4 tablespoons Parmesan cheese, grated
4 tablespoons finely chopped fresh cilantro

Cook pasta according to package directions; drain.

Add minced garlic and olive oil to the warm pasta pot. Sauté until garlic is fragrant. Add pasta back to the warm pot along with the remaining ingredients and stir until well combined. Adjust seasonings. Serve immediately.

Serves 5 as a side dish

Spinach Pesto Pasta

Flavorful and low fat, Spinach Pesto Pasta can be served as a side dish or with a bowl of soup.

1 bunch fresh spinach
Olive oil
½ cup fresh basil leaves
Salt
1 (32-ounce) package GF fettuccini (I prefer Tinkyada fettuccini)
Sundried tomatoes
4 cloves garlic, minced
4 tablespoons margarine

Cook spinach; squeeze liquid from spinach, collecting and reserving liquid. Place spinach, olive oil, basil leaves, and salt in a food processor fitted with knife blade; puree. Add sundried tomatoes and pulse until tomatoes are chopped. Set aside.

Cook pasta in reserved spinach water with extra water added; drain.

Add minced garlic and 4 tablespoon margarine to the hot pot used to cook pasta. Sauté until garlic is fragrant. Return cooked hot pasta to pot. Add spinach mixture and mix well. Add more olive oil if necessary.

Serves 6 - 8

Macaroni and Cheese

When my children could not have dairy, I would substitute Alta Dena's Raw Cow's Milk cheddar cheese and soymilk in this recipe.

1 (16-ounce) package GF brown rice pasta shells
2 tablespoons butter, margarine, or olive oil
½ cup milk
1½ cups grated Cheddar cheese
½ teaspoon salt
½ teaspoon GF Dijon mustard
Pepper, optional

Cook pasta according to package directions, being careful not to overcook. Drain pasta in colander.

While pasta is draining, add butter and margarine or olive oil to the warm pot (used to cook pasta) along with milk, grated cheese, salt, and mustard. Return hot pasta back to the pot, stirring until cheese is melted and ingredients are thoroughly combined. Adjust seasonings. Add pepper if desired.

Serves 6

Tex-Mex Mac & Cheese

1 (16-ounce) package brown rice pasta shells
1 (17-ounce) jar salsa (we prefer Amy's medium salsa)
1 (10¾-ounce) can tomato puree
1 teaspoon cumin
½ cup shopped cilantro
1 (19-ounce) can black beans, rinsed and drained
1 bunch green onions, sliced
2 cups (8-ounces) Cheddar cheese, shredded
1 cup (4-ounces) Monterey Jack cheese, shredded

Cook pasta; drain. Combine salsa and next 5 ingredients in a medium bowl, mixing well. Place half of pasta in bottom of a 13 x 9-inch baking dish sprayed with GF baking spray. Top with half of the sauce mixture, then half of the cheese; repeat. Cover with foil. Bake 350 degrees for 45 minutes. Uncover; bake 5 more minutes.

Yield: One 13 x 9-inch pan

Sesame Noodles

This is a peanut-free version of an old favorite!

1 (8-ounce) package GF brown rice spaghetti or other GF pasta
¼ cup GF soy sauce (preferably low sodium)
2 tablespoons GF sesame tahini
2 tablespoons roasted smooth almond butter
1 tablespoon brown rice vinegar
1 tablespoon lemon juice, or more to taste
1 teaspoon toasted sesame oil
1 cup shredded red cabbage
1½ cups shredded carrots
1 cup sliced green onions
1 tablespoon toasted sesame seeds

Cook pasta al dente according to package directions. Drain pasta thoroughly.

In a large bowl, whisk together soy sauce, tahini, almond butter, vinegar, lemon juice, and toasted sesame oil. Add pasta, cabbage, carrots, and green onions. Toss to coat noodles thoroughly with sauce. Sprinkle with sesame seeds and serve.

Serves 2

Soup, Stew
and
Chili

Savory Sausage and Squash Soup

Fabulous flavor and great nutrition can be offered to your family in about 45 minutes. Dairy, such as cream, can be added for a creamier base but is not necessary for a wonderful, satisfying soup.

1 large butternut squash, peeled, seeded, and cut into small cubes
1 sweet onion, chopped
1 cup chopped red bell pepper
1 pound GF fully cooked sausage link, cut into bite-size pieces
Garlic, minced
¼ teaspoon red pepper flakes
4 cups GF chicken broth
1 teaspoon dried sage
1 teaspoon granulated sugar (optional)
2 cups spinach, chopped

Bring water to a boil in a large stock pot. In the meantime, cube squash. Cook squash cubes in boiling water until squash is tender, about 10 minutes; drain. While squash is cooking chop onion, red bell pepper, and sausage. While squash is draining add onion to the stock pot and sauté until clear. Add garlic and sauté 1 minute longer.

Place onion, garlic, and drained squash in a food processor with knife blade attached; puree until smooth.

Return pureed squash mixture to stock pot and add chicken broth, sage, sugar, sausage, and chopped red bell pepper. Heat over medium heat, covered, just until soup begins to bubble, stirring occasionally. Add spinach and stir just until spinach is wilted. Serve immediately. Do not bring this soup to a boil. This soup freezes well.

Serves 4

French Onion Soup

Impress guests or treat your family to "the best" French Onion Soup. Although this recipe requires time, it can be made ahead of time and frozen. Just thaw, heat, ladle into bowls, top with a crouton and Swiss cheese, and place under the broiler until cheese is melted, for a fantastic first course.

4 tablespoons butter
2 tablespoons canola oil
2 pounds onions, thinly sliced (about 7 cups)
1 teaspoon salt
3 tablespoons sorghum flour mix
1½ quarts GF chicken broth
½ quart GF beef broth

Melt butter and oil in a heavy 4 - 5 quart stock pot over medium heat. Add onions and salt, cooking uncovered over low heat for 20 to 30 minutes, stirring occasionally, until the onions are a rich golden brown. Sprinkle flour over the onions and cook 2 to 3 minutes more, stirring constantly. Remove the pan from the heat.

In a separate saucepan bring both broths to a simmer. Stir the hot broth into the onions. Return the pot to low heat and simmer, partially covered, for another 40-50 minutes. Add salt and pepper to taste.

Croutes for onion soup:
12 - 16 (1-inch thick) slices of dried GF bread
2 teaspoons olive oil
1 garlic clove, cut
1 cup grated Swiss cheese

Preheat oven to 325 degrees. With a pastry brush, lightly coat both sides of bread with olive oil. Lay the slices of bread in a single layer on a baking sheet. Bake 15 minutes. Turn the slices over and bake another 15 minutes or until bread is completely dry and lightly brown. Rub each slice with a cut garlic clove and set aside.

To serve onion soup:
Preheat oven to 375 degrees. Ladle hot soup into ovenproof bowls. Top with a croute and grated cheese. Bake 10 - 12 minutes or until cheese has melted. Then broil for 1 minute to brown the cheese.

Big Pot Minestrone

1 onion, chopped
3 tablespoons olive oil
4 garlic cloves, minced
2 (28-ounce) cans tomato puree
1 (28-ounces) can crushed tomatoes
3 (16-ounce) cans navy beans
1 (32-ounce) carton GF chicken broth
3 large carrots, chopped into bite-size pieces
2 cups chopped fresh (or frozen) green beans
1 tablespoon dried sage
2 tablespoons dried oregano
2 tablespoons dried basil
Salt and pepper to taste

Heat a large stock pot over medium heat. Add onion and olive oil, sautéing onion until clear. Add garlic and remaining ingredients; bring to a boil. Then turn heat to low and simmer several hours.

Garnish with grated Parmesan cheese if desired.

Serves 8

Cream of Turkey and Wild Rice Soup

When cooking for the holidays, consider choosing a bigger turkey than needed since turkey lends itself well to leftovers! Meals made from leftover turkey make dinner for the next night easy on the cook. With only about 144 calories and less than 2 grams of saturated fat per 3-ounce serving, roasted turkey is healthy as well. Plus, cooked poultry is endlessly versatile. Try Turkey Divan, page 151. Spice things up by making a quick tostada with a crisp tortilla shell and creamy avocado spread another night (see Chunky Guacamole on page, 278). Or, cozy up to this wonderful soup

1 tablespoon olive oil
1 medium onion, diced or ¼ cup chopped shallots
¾ cup chopped celery
¾ cup chopped carrots
¼ cup sorghum flour mix
¼ teaspoon salt
¼ teaspoon freshly ground pepper
4 cups reduced-sodium chicken broth (or turkey broth)
1 cup instant wild rice
3 cups shredded cooked turkey or chicken (about 12-ounces)
2 cups sliced mushrooms (about 4-ounces)
½ cup reduced-fat sour cream
2 tablespoons chopped fresh parsley

Heat oil in a large stock pot over medium heat. Add onion, celery, and carrots, stirring often until softened, about 5 minutes. Stir in flour, salt, and pepper. Immediately whisk in broth and bring to a boil. Add rice, cover and simmer until rice is tender, about 45 minutes.

Stir in cooked turkey, mushrooms, sour cream, and parsley and cook until heated through, about 2 minutes.

Makes 4 servings, about 1¾ cups each

Stew for the Crew

3 pounds lean stew meat
5 carrots, chopped into bite-size pieces
2 onions, sliced
3 celery stalks, chopped into bite-size pieces
2 bay leaves
1 tablespoon pepper
3 teaspoons salt
1 (12-ounce) bottle GF beer
1 (32-ounce) carton GF beef broth
¼ cup GF spicy brown mustard

Preheat oven to 250 degrees.

Combine all ingredients in a large roaster, stirring well. Cover and bake, 5-6 hours. Adjust salt and pepper.

Serves 12

Karen's Slow-Cooker Stew

Tender chicken, delicious flavor, and the ease of the slow cooker,
make this a great choice to serve family or guests on a cold evening.

8 chicken breasts fillets cut into 3 or 4 pieces each
½ cup sorghum flour
½ cup cornstarch
Salt and pepper
Olive oil
6 bacon slices
1 large yellow onion, thinly sliced
2 pounds new potatoes cut into bite-size pieces
1 pound mushrooms
6 garlic cloves, minced
1½ teaspoons dried thyme
1 bay leaf
1 (28-ounce) carton chicken broth
2½ cups chardonnay wine

Heat a large sauté pan over medium-high heat.

In a medium bowl, combine flour and cornstarch, salt, and pepper. Add the chicken and toss evenly to coat. Add 2 tablespoons olive oil to pan and then one half of the chicken; browning on all sides, 3 to 4 minutes total. Transfer to a slow cooker. Repeat with 2 more tablespoons olive oil and remaining chicken. Transfer remaining browned chicken to the slow cooker.

Add bacon slices and remaining ingredients to the slow cooker, cooking at high setting for 45 minutes. Then turn the slow cooker to low setting and cook for 6-7 hours more.

Serves 8

No-Peek Stew

Perfect for cold days, simply mix up this stew, cover, and bake.
For a stew recipe without tomatoes, see Winter Stew, page 245.

4 pounds lean stew meat
6 large carrots, chopped into bite-size pieces
1 - 2 onions, sliced
1½ cups celery, chopped
9 medium red potatoes, cut into large chunks
2 (28-ounce) cans diced organic tomatoes
Use the empty can from the diced tomatoes to add ½ can water
3 tablespoons dry tapioca granules (this is your thickening agent)
3 tablespoons granulated sugar
5 teaspoons salt
4 teaspoons pepper

Combine all ingredients in a large Dutch oven, stirring well. Cover and bake 250 degrees for 5 - 6 hours; no need to stir or peek!

Serves 10 (or 5 people twice!)

Zucchini Potato Soup

Smooth and creamy Zucchini Potato Soup can be served hot or cold.

1 tablespoon olive oil
1 medium onion, chopped
5 garlic cloves, minced
6 medium zucchini, cut into chunks
3 large baking potatoes, peeled and cut into chunks
2 cups water
1 teaspoon salt

Boil zucchini and potatoes in a large stock pot until tender; drain. Add olive oil and onion to stock pot. Sauté over medium heat until onion is clear. Add garlic and sauté until fragrant, about 1 minute. Place sautéed onion and garlic in a blender. Puree potato and zucchini in batches (do not fill blender more than halfway), adding water gradually to each batch. Return each pureed batch to stock pot. Add salt and season to taste. Simmer until ready to serve. Or, to serve as a cold soup, seal and refrigerate until chilled.

Serves 4

Winter Stew

4 pounds lean stew meat
5 large carrots, chopped into bite-size pieces
6 – 8 medium Yukon Gold potatoes, chopped into bite-size pieces
3 garlic cloves, minced
2 large onions, sliced
3 cups apple cider
1½ cups GF chicken broth
1 tablespoon thyme
1 tablespoon crushed rosemary
¼ cup parsley, chopped
2 – 3 tablespoons cornstarch

Place meat and chopped vegetables in a large roaster. Stir cornstarch into 1 cup broth and whisk until well combined. Add broth mixture to roaster, stirring well. Bake 275 - 300 degrees, 6 - 8 hours.

Serves 8

Soup for Sick Days

This is our family's favorite soup for a quicker recovery from colds or flu.

3 garlic cloves, minced
1 medium onion, chopped
2 tablespoons olive oil
1 (32-ounce) carton organic vegetable broth
1 (32-ounce) carton organic chicken broth
2 large carrots, grated
2 celery stalks, chopped fine
1 medium red bell pepper, chopped (optional)
2 teaspoons dried basil or 2 teaspoons crushed dried rosemary
1 cup uncooked quinoa

In a large pot, sauté garlic and onion in olive oil for 2 minutes. Add other ingredients and bring to a boil. Reduce heat to low, partially cover, and simmer for two hours.

Makes about 8 servings…can be frozen in small portions

Baked Potato Soup

4 large baking potatoes
¾ cup butter or margarine
¾ cup sorghum flour mix
6 cups milk
¾ teaspoon salt
½ teaspoon pepper
4 green onions, chopped and divided
12 slices bacon, cooked, crumbled, and divided
1¼ cups (5-ounces) shredded Cheddar cheese, divided
1 (8-ounce) carton sour cream

Wash potatoes and prick several times with a fork. Bake potatoes at 400 degrees for 1 hour or until done; cool at room temperature. Cut potatoes in half lengthwise, then scoop out pulp; set aside. Discard potato skins or reserve for Crisp Potato Skins. Melt butter in a heavy saucepan over low heat. Add the flour, stirring until smooth. Gradually add milk and cook over medium heat, whisking constantly, until mixture is thickened and bubbles. Add potato pulp, salt, pepper, 2 tablespoons green onions, ½ cup bacon, and 1 cup cheese. Cook until thoroughly heated; add extra milk if necessary for desired thickness. When desired thickness is reached, stir in sour cream and serve immediately with remaining onion, bacon, and cheese.

Serves 4-6

Potato Corn Chowder
with Edamame

This easy, tasty recipe incorporates edamame (shelled baby soybeans) to pack a punch of protein to this meatless meal. Read more about edamame's nutritional value on page 277 under Edamame Spread, a quick, easy, and delicious spread for crackers, veggies, or corn tortilla chips.

1 medium onion, chopped
2 stalks celery, chopped
1 red bell pepper, chopped
5 cups GF chicken broth
3 cups milk
1 (16-ounce) package frozen corn
1 (16-ounce) package frozen edamame
½ teaspoon dried thyme
6 small white potatoes, peeled and cubed
Salt to taste
1 teaspoon pepper
5 slices bacon, cooked and crumbled
Grated Cheddar cheese

Add first three ingredients to a large stock pot and sauté for several minutes. Add broth, milk, frozen corn, frozen edamame, thyme, and potatoes. Add about ½ to 2 teaspoons salt (depending on taste and whether or not your broth was salted) and 1 teaspoon pepper. Simmer several hours, until potatoes are tender.

Ladle into soup bowls and top with grated Cheddar cheese and crumbled bacon bits.

Makes 8 cups of soup

Bison Chili

Fire-roasted tomatoes, chipotle pepper seasoning, and sweet corn, combine to make this great chili. Ground bison is leaner than ground sirloin making it a very healthy choice for meat dishes, but you can substitute lean ground beef for the ground bison if you choose.

2 pounds ground bison or ground sirloin
1 medium onion, chopped
1 teaspoon salt
½ teaspoon pepper
3 garlic cloves, minced
1 (28-ounce) can tomato puree
1 (28-ounce) can water
1 (28-ounce) can fire-roasted diced tomatoes
1 (6-ounce) can tomato paste
1 (16-ounce) bag frozen corn
2½ teaspoons chipotle seasoning powder
2 teaspoons chili seasoning powder

In large pot, brown meat with onion; season with salt and pepper; drain fat. Add garlic cloves and remaining ingredients. Simmer several hours or transfer to a slow cooker and cook on low for 6 hours. Serve with grated cheddar and tortilla chips.

Serves 6

Vegetable Chili

Though I don't care to become a vegetarian and give up a juicy burger hot off the grill, I have begun to serve my family more meatless meals in an effort to reduce saturated fat and cholesterol. Serve a hearty, tasty chili like this one and your family won't even notice that the meat is missing. Place all ingredients in a large stock pot and allow it to simmer 4-5 hours, or try cooking it in a slow-cooker. Serve with Quinoa Cornbread Muffins, page 53, for a meal packed with nutrition.

3 large carrots, diced
2 celery ribs, diced
1 large onion, diced
2 large zucchini, chopped
2 yellow crookneck squash, chopped
1 tablespoon chili powder
1 teaspoon dried basil
1 teaspoon pepper
1 (6-ounce) can tomato paste
4 cups low sodium tomato juice
2 (14½-ounce) cans diced tomatoes, undrained
4 (15-ounce) cans pinto, or great Northern beans, rinsed and drained
1 cup frozen whole kernel corn

Combine all ingredients in large stock pot or slow cooker and simmer for at least 3 hours. After veggies are tender, adjust seasonings according to taste.

Serves 5-6

Condensed Cream Soup

This recipe can be used as a substitute for one 10¾-ounce can
of condensed Cream of Mushroom, Cream of Celery,
or Cream of Chicken soup.

1 cup cold milk
2 tablespoons cornstarch
1½ tablespoons butter
1 teaspoon chicken bouillon
½ teaspoon salt
Dash pepper

In a small saucepan, whisk milk and cornstarch until well blended. Stir in butter, bouillon, salt and pepper. Heat to boiling, stirring frequently. Simmer on low 1 minute longer to thicken.

Condensed Cream of Mushroom Soup:
Stir in one 4-ounce can of mushroom pieces, drained.

Condensed Cream of Chicken Soup:
Stir in ½ cup cooked chicken pieces.

Condensed Cream of Celery Soup:
Stir in ½ cup sautéed chopped celery.

Salads
and
Dressing

Delicious Chicken Salad

This recipe makes great use of leftover chicken breasts.

Dressing:
1 cup mayonnaise
4 teaspoons lemon juice
5 teaspoons honey
2 teaspoons poppy seeds
Salt and pepper to taste

Prepare the dressing by thoroughly mixing together all dressing ingredients in a jar; refrigerate.

Salad:
3 cups boneless cooked chicken breast pieces
¾ cup pecan pieces, toasted
1 cup red seedless grapes, halved
3 stalks celery, thinly sliced

Combine all ingredients in a medium bowl. Add the dressing and stir well. Refrigerate until ready to serve.

Serves 6

Grilled Chicken Salad with Lemon-Mint Vinaigrette

1 tablespoon hot paprika
1½ teaspoons minced garlic
½ teaspoon dried oregano
½ teaspoon ground cumin
½ cup plus ¼ cup olive oil
Salt and pepper
2 tablespoons chopped parsley
2 tablespoons chopped fresh mint
2 tablespoons fresh lemon juice
2 teaspoons grated lemon zest
¼ teaspoon cayenne pepper
2 pounds skinless, boneless chicken breasts, cut into chunks
1 large red onion, sliced crosswise ½ inch thick
8 cups loosely packed washed arugula or spinach
Lemon wedges, optional

Preheat a grill to medium-hot.

In a small bowl, mix the paprika with 1 teaspoon of the garlic, the oregano, and the cumin. Whisk in ½ cup of the olive oil and season the paprika oil with salt and pepper.

In another bowl, combine the parsley, mint, lemon juice, lemon zest, cayenne and the remaining ½ teaspoon of garlic. Whisk in the remaining ¼ cup of the olive oil and season the vinaigrette with salt and pepper.

Thread the chicken pieces onto 6 skewers. Brush the chicken and onion slices all over with the paprika oil and arrange on the grill. Cook the onions for 4 minutes, turning once, until they are slightly softened. Grill the chicken for 12 minutes, turning occasionally, until it is cooked through.

Arrange the arugula or spinach on a platter. Spread the onions and chicken on top, drizzle with the vinaigrette and serve with lemon wedges.

Serves 6

Chunky Chicken Parmesan Salad

4 cups chopped cooked chicken breast
½ cup light GF mayonnaise
¼ cup freshly shredded Parmesan cheese
2 green onions, chopped
2 celery ribs, chopped
2 tablespoons chopped pecans, toasted
¼ teaspoon pepper
¼ teaspoon salt

Stir together all ingredients. Cover and chill 2 hours.

Serves 4-6

Citrus Salad with Candied Pumpkin Seeds

3 tablespoons orange juice
2 tablespoons fresh lemon juice
½ teaspoon granulated sugar
½ teaspoon cumin
¼ teaspoon salt
¼ teaspoon pepper
½ cup olive oil
Mixed salad greens
Candied Pumpkin Seeds, page 128

Combine orange juice, lemon juice, sugar, cumin, salt, pepper, and olive oil in a jar, seal tightly with lid and shake well. Assemble salad greens, top with desired amount of pumpkin seeds, pour dressing over, and toss. Serve immediately.

Yield: ½ cup dressing

Quinoa with Grilled Vegetables

*Read more about quinoa's "super food" qualities on page 16.
And be sure to try Quinoa with a Kick on page 229, Warm Quinoa Spinach
Salad on page 259, and one of my family's favorites,
Quinoa Cornbread on page 53.*

1 cup quinoa, uncooked
2 cups vegetable stock or water
1 cup grilled vegetables
1 tablespoon Parmesan cheese, grated

Marinade:
¼ cup olive oil
¼ teaspoon dried basil
¼ teaspoon dried oregano
¼ teaspoon dried thyme
¼ teaspoon dried rosemary, crushed
1 clove garlic, chopped

Grilled Vegetables:
1 medium zucchini, cut lengthwise
1 medium yellow squash, cut lengthwise
3 Roma tomatoes cut lengthwise
1 tablespoon garlic cloves, roasted
1 tablespoon shallots, roasted

Combine all marinade ingredients in a zip-top bag or large bowl. Add the zucchini, squash, and tomatoes to the marinade, mixing to coat thoroughly. Let sit 30 minutes or up to 2 hours. Roast the garlic and shallots, 8-10 minutes at 350; let cool, then chop coarsely. Remove vegetables from the marinade and grill over medium-high heat, let cool, then cut into 1-inch pieces.

To cook the quinoa, rinse grain in colander under cold water to remove naturally occurring resin; drain. Combine with stock or water in a pot. Simmer over medium heat for about 20 minutes or until all liquid is absorbed. Toss cooked quinoa, grilled vegetables, roasted garlic & shallots, and Parmesan cheese in a bowl. Serve immediately.

Thai-Style Steak Salad

Easy and fabulously delicious! See photo on insert page F.

¼ cup fresh lime juice
1 tablespoon GF soy sauce
1 tablespoon granulated sugar
¼ to ½ teaspoon red pepper flakes
3 tablespoons canola oil
Salt and pepper to taste
2 to 3 large carrots, grated
1 large head romaine lettuce
½ cup fresh mint leaves, chopped
One (1-inch thick) slab of GF deli roast beef

Slice roast beef very thin, cutting against the grain. Combine lime juice and next 5 ingredients in a jar. Seal jar and shake well. Tear lettuce into a large salad bowl, top with grated carrots, mint leaves, and strips of beef. Pour dressing over salad, mix well, and serve immediately.

Serves 4-5

Honey-Mustard Potato Salad

A great picnic salad or complement for grilled meats…

10 small red potatoes cut into bite-size pieces
¼ cup chopped green onions
1 to 2 large celery stalks, chopped
1 medium red bell pepper, chopped
3 tablespoons GF Dijon mustard
Juice from one lemon
3 tablespoons honey
1 teaspoon salt
1 teaspoon pepper

Boil potatoes just until tender; cool. Meanwhile, whisk the mustard, lemon juice, honey, salt, and pepper in a large bowl. Toss in potatoes, green onion, celery, and red pepper. Refrigerate until ready to serve or serve warm.

Asian Cabbage Salad
with Spicy Peanut Sauce

This very tasty salad provides a great accompaniment to an Asian dinner or,wrap the tossed salad in rice wrappers for a lunch or dinner to go.

8 cups thinly sliced Napa cabbage
1 cup loosely packed, roughly chopped cilantro leaves
3 scallions, thinly sliced
1 medium carrot, grated
1 cup toasted peanuts, chopped

For salad:
In a large salad bowl, toss together cabbage, cilantro, scallions, and carrot. Toss in peanuts. Add dressing and toss until evenly distributed. Taste and adjust seasonings. Serve immediately.

For dressing:
Combine all of the ingredients below in a glass bowl and whisk until well combined.

1 teaspoon sesame oil
3 tablespoons rice wine vinegar
¼ cup low sodium GF soy sauce
2 tablespoons granulated sugar or 2 tablespoons agave nectar
1 tablespoon freshly grated ginger
½ teaspoon red pepper flakes

Serves 6

Watergate Salad

Don't forget this old favorite which can easily be made gluten-free.

1 (20-ounce) can crushed pineapple with juice
1 (3-ounce) package instant pistachio pudding mix
1 (8-ounce) carton GF non-dairy whipped topping
1 cup GF mini marshmallows (optional)
1 cup nuts

Fold pudding into crushed pineapple. Add other ingredients. Refrigerate until ready to serve.

Serves 6-8

Cranberry Spinach Salad

1 tablespoon butter
¾ cup slivered almonds
1 pound fresh spinach
1 cup dried cranberries
1 tablespoon poppy seeds
¼ cup granulated sugar
2 teaspoons green onion, chopped
¼ teaspoon paprika
¼ cup white wine vinegar
½ cup extra virgin olive oil
Dash of salt

Melt butter in a medium saucepan. Add almonds and cook until toasted.

In a large bowl tear 1 pound of fresh spinach into bite-sized pieces, topping with almonds and cranberries.

Combine poppy seeds and remaining ingredients in a jar, seal, and shake well. Pour desired amount over salad, toss, and serve immediately.

Warm Quinoa
Spinach Salad

This 500 year-old grain originated in Peru where it is still widely used as food and referred to as the "mother grain" since it is self-perpetuating and ever bearing. Not technically a grain, quinoa is most closely related to spinach and beets. It is high in phosphorus, calcium, iron, vitamin C and B, as well as fiber and protein. It is also packed with lysine and other amino acids that make a protein complete, resulting in superb nutrition for anyone, not just Celiacs.

½ cup red-wine vinegar
¼ cup plus 2 tablespoons olive oil
Coarse salt and ground pepper
1½ cups quinoa, rinsed in a fine mesh strainer
1 pound baby spinach
8 ounces Feta cheese, crumbled, or shredded Mozzarella cheese

In a small bowl, whisk together vinegar, oil, ½ teaspoon salt, and ¼ teaspoon pepper.

Meanwhile, combine quinoa, 3 cups water, and 1 teaspoon salt in a saucepan. Bring to a boil; reduce heat to medium-low and simmer until liquid has been absorbed.

Place spinach in a large bowl; add cooked quinoa and dressing, tossing to combine (spinach will wilt slightly). Top with crumbled Feta or shredded Mozzarella cheese.

Summer Corn Salad

Roasted corn provides this perfect recipe for a weekend barbeque
or a quick side dish for leftovers.

5 ears roasted corn, husked and kernels removed
2 plum tomatoes, seeded and finely chopped
¼ cup avocado, finely chopped
3 tablespoons pine nuts, lightly toasted
2 tablespoons chopped parsley
3 tablespoons white balsamic vinegar
¼ cup olive oil
Salt and pepper to taste

To roast corn, remove outer husks. Turn back inner husks; remove silk. Replace inner husks. Grill 12-15 minutes over medium-high heat, turning often. Husks will be charred but corn will be delicious.

Place corn, tomatoes, avocados, pine nuts, and parsley in a bowl. Pour the vinegar and olive oil over the ingredients. Gently toss; season with salt and pepper. Cover and chill for at least one hour.

Serves 4

Berry Blue Salad

A super, summer salad when berries are perfect and plentiful.

8 cups loosely packed baby greens
½ cup fresh blueberries
½ cup thinly sliced red onion
½ cup olive oil
½ cup orange juice
1 tablespoon fresh lemon thyme leaves
Salt and pepper
¼ cup roasted sliced almonds

Place greens, blueberries, and red onion in a serving bowl. In a smaller bowl, whisk together olive oil, orange juice, and lemon thyme leaves. Toss greens with dressing and garnish with almonds; season with salt and pepper to taste.   Serve immediately.

Serves 4

Tropical Salad

½ cup GF mayonnaise
¼ cup canola oil
¼ cup chopped green onion
2 tablespoons honey
3 tablespoons fresh lemon juice
1 tablespoon chopped fresh parsley
¼ teaspoon prepared GF mustard
1 large head iceberg lettuce or 1 large head romaine lettuce
1 green pepper, thinly sliced
½ small cucumber
1 (4½ -ounce) can small shrimp, rinsed and drained
¼ cup chopped walnuts

Combine the first 7 ingredients in the container of an electric blender, or in a food processor fitted with the knife blade. Process until smooth; chill.

Tear lettuce into bite-size pieces in a salad bowl. Add remaining ingredients; toss well. Serve with the reserved chilled dressing.

Yield: 8 servings

Fresh Italian Dressing

1 teaspoon garlic powder
2 teaspoons granulated sugar
2 teaspoons dried mustard
Salt and pepper
½ teaspoon crushed red pepper flakes
¼ cup plus 2 tablespoons red wine vinegar
½ cup extra virgin olive oil
¼ cup fresh chopped basil
1 teaspoon fresh chopped oregano

Whisk garlic, sugar, mustard, 1½ teaspoons salt, ½ teaspoon pepper, red pepper flakes, and vinegar in a medium bowl. Whisk together oils; add to the vinegar mixture in a slow steady stream, whisking until emulsified. Whisk in herbs. Adjust salt and pepper. Refrigerate in an airtight container up to 1 week.

Makes 1½ cups

Warm Pecan Dressing

Serve over mixed greens for a Southerner's delight!

2 tablespoons balsamic vinegar
2 teaspoons honey
1 tablespoon GF Dijon mustard
½ cup coarsely chopped pecans
2 teaspoons canola oil

Combine all ingredients in a small saucepan. Heat mixture over medium heat until warm. Pour over mixed greens; serve immediately.

Lemon Basil Dressing

¼ cup mayonnaise
½ cup fresh basil leaves
Juice from ½ of a lemon
¼ cup olive oil
1 tablespoon honey
Dash pepper
Dash salt

Combine all ingredients in food processor, fitted with the knife blade. Pulse until basil is chopped and ingredients are well blended.

Yield: ½ cup

French Dressing

¼ cup white-wine vinegar
¼ cup ketchup
1 tablespoon sugar, honey, or agave nectar
2 teaspoons paprika
1 teaspoon Worcestershire sauce
Coarse salt
¼ cup plus 3 tablespoons olive oil

In a small bowl, whisk together vinegar, ketchup, sugar, paprika, and Worcestershire; season with salt. Whisking constantly, add the oil in a steady stream until incorporated.

Yield: ¾ cup

Basic Vinaigrette

True vinaigrette has more oil than vinegar.
The mustard in this recipe flavors, as well as thickens, the dressing.

¼ cup white wine vinegar
1 tablespoon GF Dijon mustard
Pinch sugar or ½ teaspoon agave nectar
Coarse sugar and ground pepper
¾ cup extra virgin olive oil

In a small bowl, whisk together vinegar, mustard, and sugar; season with salt and pepper. Slowly add oil, whisking to combine, or shake all ingredients in a jar.

Yield: 1 cup

Ginger Mint Balsamic Dressing

¼ cup olive oil
¼ cup balsamic vinegar
¼ cup white wine vinegar
1 tablespoon GF Dijon mustard
1 tablespoon fresh grated ginger
2 tablespoons honey
1 teaspoon garlic powder
1 tablespoon chopped mint
Grind of fresh pepper
Pinch of salt

Whisk all ingredients in a medium bowl. Serve over mixed greens.

Yield: ¾ cup

Sauce
and
Salsa

CHAPTER 21

Butternut Squash Pasta Sauce

Pureed butternut squash can be added to soups or your favorite tomato sauce recipe so it is cleverly disguised. However, this recipe has nothing to hide with its appealing color and delicious flavor. It also provides a creamy, satisfying pasta dish without the tomato sauce, for those who avoid night-shade vegetables.

1 medium butternut squash (about 1½ pounds)
1 tablespoon olive oil
½ teaspoon dried rubbed sage
Salt and pepper
5 garlic cloves, peel on
1 cup half-and-half (or chicken broth for a non-dairy version)
Pasta
Toppings such as fresh chopped herbs or grated cheese

Preheat oven to 375 degrees. Using a large, sharp knife, trim ends; halve squash crosswise to separate bulb from neck. Peel with a vegetable peeler. Cut both pieces in half lengthwise. Scoop out seeds with a spoon; discard.

Cut squash into 2-inch chunks; transfer to a small rimmed baking sheet. Toss with oil and sage; season with salt and pepper. Scatter garlic around squash. Roast until squash is very tender, about 40 minutes, tossing once halfway through. Remove and discard skin from garlic.

Transfer squash and garlic to a food processor; puree. With motor running, add half-and-half through the feed tube; process until smooth. Add 1 to 2 cups water; continue to process until smooth, adding water to thin if necessary. Adjust seasonings.

Cook pasta according to package directions. Drain pasta and return to pot. Pour sauce over pasta; serve immediately. Garnish as desired.

Yield: About 4 cups

Leftover cooled sauce can be frozen in airtight containers for up to 3 months.

Pumpkin Seed
Tomatillo Sauce

Serve this warm sauce over grilled chicken and rice, use it in an enchilada recipe, or serve it cold as a salsa with tortilla chips. Pumpkin seeds are a great source of magnesium, manganese, phosphorus, iron, copper, protein, and zinc. They are thought to reduce blood cholesterol, increase bone mineral density, and may help males maintain prostate health.

1½ cups raw green pumpkin seeds
½ pound fresh tomatillos
½ cup chopped sweet onion
2 tablespoons chopped garlic
2 fresh green Serrano chiles, coarsely chopped (including seeds)
1 teaspoon salt (or to taste)
1 cup chopped fresh cilantro, divided
¼ cup corn oil

Heat a wide heavy pot over moderate heat until hot, about 5 minutes, then toast pumpkin seeds, stirring constantly, until puffed and beginning to pop, 3-6 minutes. Transfer seeds to a plate to cool.

Grind pumpkin seeds to a fine powder in grinder or food processor, and then stir together with 2 cups water.

Heat the oil in the pot, over moderate heat, until hot but not smoking. Then add the pumpkin seed mixture and cook, stirring constantly, until thickened.

Discard husks from tomatillos and rinse tomatillos under warm water to remove any stickiness. Coarsely chop tomatillos, then puree in a food processor with onion, garlic, chiles, salt, ½ cup cilantro, and ½ cup water until very smooth.

Add tomatillo puree to pumpkin seeds and simmer, stirring, 2 minutes. Continue to simmer, uncovered, about 15 minutes longer, stirring occasionally. Before serving, add ½ cup chopped cilantro.

Makes about 6 cups

White Sauce

This basic white sauce is great for pasta or rice.
You can add white wine, chopped fresh basil, minced garlic,
or chopped tomatoes for other variations.

2 tablespoons olive oil
¼ cup butter or margarine
¼ cup sorghum flour mix or sweet white rice flour
2 cups milk
Salt

Place olive oil and butter or margarine in small saucepan. Heat over medium-high heat until butter is melted. Add flour, stirring with a wire whisk. Whisk in milk gradually. Add salt to taste.

Salsa Fresca

The taste of fresh ingredients in this salsa beats the jarred versions
by a mile, however it is at its best for only a short while.
Keep it chilled and use within a day.
This salsa is great served over Cowboy Hash, page 31.

1 cup seeded and diced Roma tomatoes
¼ cup minced onion
2 tablespoons diced green bell pepper
1 tablespoon minced jalapeno
1 tablespoon olive oil
1 garlic clove, minced
2 teaspoons chopped fresh cilantro
½ teaspoon oregano
1 tablespoon fresh lime juice
½ teaspoon salt
¼ teaspoon pepper

Combine the tomatoes, onion, green pepper, jalapeno, olive oil, garlic, cilantro, and oregano. Add lime juice, salt, and pepper to taste.

Let the salsa rest in a covered container in the refrigerator at least 30 minutes before serving.

Makes about 1½ cups

No-Tomato Sauce

*This recipe is from a mailing list to which I subscribe,
contributed for those who cannot have nightshade vegetables due to the
arthritic symptoms associated with Celiac Disease.
You won't believe it's not really tomatoes, and it is easy to make.
Use it as pizza sauce, chili base, or spaghetti sauce.*

¾ cup onion, chopped
1 clove garlic, minced
2½ cups carrots, sliced
½ cup beets, sliced
¾ cup water
3 tablespoons lemon juice
1½ teaspoon salt
1 tablespoon dried basil
¼ teaspoon dried oregano

Brown onion and garlic in a small saucepan. Place onion and garlic in a
blender. In the same saucepan, steam carrots and beets until tender. Add
the carrots, beets, and remaining ingredients to the blender with the onion
and garlic; blend until smooth.

For Spaghetti Sauce: Stir cooked ground meat into the sauce.
For Chili: Omit the basil and season sauce with chili seasonings such as
cumin, chili powder, or Mexican seasoning blend.
For Marinara Sauce: Add ¼ cup olive oil, 1 tablespoon balsamic vinegar,
and 2 tablespoons red wine to the sauce.

Make a double batch and freeze in canning jars, leaving 1-inch of space
for sauce to expand.

Classic Tartar Sauce

½ cup mayonnaise
2 tablespoons minced red onion
2 tablespoons sweet pickle relish
2 tablespoons minced fresh parsley
2 teaspoons fresh lemon juice

In a small bowl, stir all ingredients together. Cover and refrigerate until
needed. Sauce will keep for up to one week.

Quick Warm Blueberry Sauce

Made with fresh or frozen blueberries, this homemade sauce is a tasty alternative to the classic Maple syrup pancake topping.
It is also great to spoon atop yogurt, biscuits, pound cake, or ice cream.

2½ cups fresh or frozen blueberries (not in juice)
½ cup granulated sugar
½ cup orange juice
1 tablespoon cornstarch
2 teaspoons lemon juice

Combine the blueberries, sugar, and ¼ cup of the orange juice in a medium-size saucepan. Warm the mixture over moderate heat, stirring it occasionally.

As the berries heat, blend the cornstarch into the remaining orange juice, using the back of a spoon to dissolve any lumps.

Increase the heat and bring the sauce to a boil. Stir the cornstarch mixture again and then add it to the fruit. Cook the sauce at a low boil for 1 minute, stirring constantly.

Remove the pan from the heat and stir in the lemon juice. Cool the sauce for 5 to 10 minutes before serving (it will thicken as it cools).

Yield: About 2 cups

Dips
and
Spreads

Pick your Pesto

*When summer provides you with abundant basil, make pesto!
Choose a variety, place the ingredients in a food processor fitted with the
knife blade and process until smooth, stopping to scrape down the sides.
Harvest your basil at the end of summer making big batches of pesto,
spoon into ice cube trays, and freeze. Once frozen, the pesto cubes can be
popped-out into a freezer zip-top bag and returned to the freezer for
use all winter. Pesto cubes can be added to a pasta sauce or thawed and
spread on a pizza, used on pasta, in salad dressings, or as a dip.*

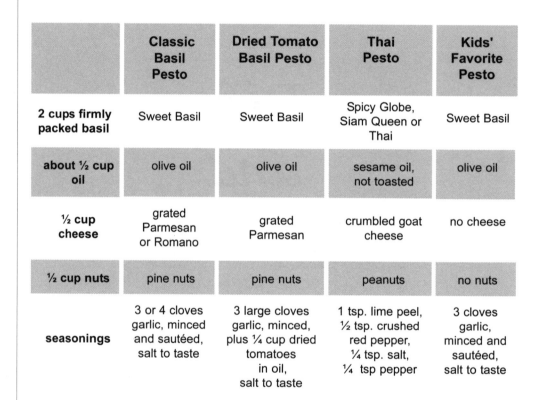

	Classic Basil Pesto	Dried Tomato Basil Pesto	Thai Pesto	Kids' Favorite Pesto
2 cups firmly packed basil	Sweet Basil	Sweet Basil	Spicy Globe, Siam Queen or Thai	Sweet Basil
about ½ cup oil	olive oil	olive oil	sesame oil, not toasted	olive oil
½ cup cheese	grated Parmesan or Romano	grated Parmesan	crumbled goat cheese	no cheese
½ cup nuts	pine nuts	pine nuts	peanuts	no nuts
seasonings	3 or 4 cloves garlic, minced and sautéed, salt to taste	3 large cloves garlic, minced, plus ¼ cup dried tomatoes in oil, salt to taste	1 tsp. lime peel, ½ tsp. crushed red pepper, ¼ tsp. salt, ¼ tsp pepper	3 cloves garlic, minced and sautéed, salt to taste